THE LAST
OF THE
HIPPIES

THE LAST OF THE HIPPIES

An Hysterical Romance

Penny Rimbaud

The Last of the Hippies: An Hysterical Romance
© Penny Rimbaud
This edition copyright ©2015 PM Press
All Rights Reserved

ISBN: 9781629631035
Library of Congress Control Number: 2015930877

PM Press
PO Box 23912
Oakland, CA 94623
www.pmpress.org

Previously published in the UK by Active Distribution
www.activedistribution.org

Cover by John Yates/stealworks.com

10 9 8 7 6 5 4 3 2 1

Printed by the Employee Owners of Thomson-Shore in Dexter, Michigan.
www.thomsonshore.com

In loving memory of John Loder

INTRODUCTION

*'When I hear the word 'culture', I reach for
my revolver.'*

—Hermann Goering

IT'S PROBABLY FIFTEEN YEARS SINCE I READ *THE LAST OF
the Hippies*, and it's over twenty five since I wrote it. It was
1982. That's a quarter of a century ago, pre Miners' Strike,
pre CDs, pre AIDS, pre micro-computers, pre Greenham
Women, pre crop circles, pre Battle of the Beanfield, pre
Gulf Wars One and Two, pre Bush'n'Blair, pre Seattle, pre
Globalisation (in those days we simply called it rampant
capitalism), pre 9/11, but, more important than anything
else, pre my Senior Citizen's Bus Pass. The list could go on.

When in 1977 the Sex Pistols harped on about anarchy in the UK, it became pretty obvious to me that their
interest was not in revolution but in their bank balance.

Anarchists on EMI? I think not. Likewise, when the Clash were claiming to be oh so bored with the USA, how come they were so busy booking flights to the land of plenty? Sorry, boys, you were a joke from the start, and not a very funny one at that. But take a look at any musical publication which claims to document that era and you'll be told that these guys created a cultural revolution called 'punk'. In truth, they were just another flash in the toilet pan of the great rock'n'roll circus, confirmation of the endemic cynicism of the eighties. Pretty vacant? That's for sure.

Within the populist history of rock'n'roll, the very real movement of protest which grew out of the initial punk hype and which came to be known (more by the media than by its purveyors) as 'anarcho-punk' is studiously ignored. It was no different even during its heyday, but despite the efforts both of the music business and of Thatcher's neo-Nazi Government to pretend it wasn't happening, anarcho-punk grew to become a very real threat to the status quo. Its heritage lives on today.

Crass, the anarchist punk band of which I was a founding member, drummer, lyricist and big mouth, can reasonably claim to be the initiators of anarcho-punk. We saw Johnny Rotten's 'no future' rantings as a challenge. We believed that there was a future if we were prepared to fight for it, and fight for it we did. Following the release of our 1977 album, *The Feeding of the Five Thousand*, we spearheaded a radical protest movement that had no parallel in late twentieth century Britain. Crass and fellow anarchist bands put words into action, and encouraged a whole generation to do the same.

The late seventies and early eighties were a bleak period: unemployment, collapsing social services, nuclear proliferation, war in the Falklands, the miners' battle against Thatcher's determination to destroy working class dignity, extensive deployment of the American war-machine onto British soil, in fact, globalisation in its infancy. The Thatcher/Reagan knot had been tied and it was we, the people, who were expected to accept suffocation as it tightened.

As anarcho-punk progressively proved the authenticity of its intent, so its real value as a network of radicals and activists superseded any of the considerable muscle it had as a musical genre. Nonetheless, that didn't stop it occasionally making it into the national music charts (even if the following week it would in all probability have mysteriously disappeared). While record sales boomed, the media, the music business, MI5, MI6 and Thatcher's Government made increasingly vain attempts to ignore the fast-growing movement. However, as most anarchist punks were just as happy tearing down the barbed wire fences of military bases as they might be going to a gig, it became increasingly difficult for those in power to dismiss them. The crunch came with the Stop the City riots of '83 and '84 in which thousands of punks took to the streets of the City of London with the singular aim of stopping business as usual. Their efforts were staggeringly successful, inspiring generations of street activists and leading to the massive anti-globalisation protests of the present day. From the outset, the authorities have been unamused. Thirty years on they still are and, despite the fact that they no longer exist as a working group, Crass are still under surveillance.

For all this, it should be remembered that the anarcho-punk movement was not a beginning as much as a continuation. Before that there'd been the hippies, the beats, the bohemians, right back to the beginnings of human consciousness. There's nothing new about social dissent, but unless it is willing to adapt to the times and to offer something radical and new in itself, it can become as rigid as that which it claims to oppose (which is one good reason why today, in 2008, I so loathe the fad for retro-punk).

We all know the System stinks. We all know we can stop it for a day, or even two. We all know that McDonalds and Coca-Cola are crap. We all know that wars kill. We all know that one day we are happy and the next day we might be sad. We all tell lies which we hope are truths. We all tell truths which we know are lies. What we don't yet seem to get a handle on is how once and for all we can change all that.

Thirty years ago, anarcho-punk broke a lot of new ground, not least in learning that oppositional politics tend to do little more than strengthen the opposition. The enemy within is an essential element of the oppressive State, it gives licence to erode what little civil liberties might still exist. Just look at the plethora of new anti-terrorist laws following 9/11, each and every one designed not only to challenge righteous global resistance to Western capitalist dominance, but also to legitimise the further oppression of each and every one of us, law abiding citizens or not. If not through our gullet, how else do you imagine ID cards will find their way into our wallets or micro-chip tags into our flesh?

Anarcho-punk demonstrated that there are ways of circumventing the status quo, but as it becomes increasingly obvious that corporate reality belongs to a different planet to the people in the streets, it is perhaps time to look for ways of irrevocably dislocating ourselves from it. For most of us, our relationship with commodity culture is one of love/hate. Somewhere down the line, at one time or another, all of us are guilty of 'buying in', be it a car journey we don't really need to make, a newspaper we simply must read or the cut-price supermarket beans which are just too, too cheap to be resisted. It's a tough one, but if we're truly going to beat the beast, it's one that we have to consider very seriously indeed. Regrettably, we can't have our cake and eat it. We need to create new modes of communication, new visions of change, new ways of breaking the impasse. In short, we need to create a new language. If we are to escape from the insanity of the New World Order and its globalised wonderland, we've got to reinvent ourselves in our own image. Only then will we be truly able to know what we mean and to mean what we say. Further to this, we've also got to be considerably more aware of just who it is we're talking to. We should have learnt by now that there's no point shouting into the ears of corpses. The days of politics are ended.

In 1982, Crass were at the height of their infamy. We'd spent the first part of that year in the studio, recording the double album *Christ – The Album*, probably the most carefully considered and produced record that we ever made. By then our sales were massive, so we could afford to take our time. When I wasn't in the studio, I was working on *The Last of the Hippies* which was to be included as part of the album's final packaging. For all the angst expressed both in the album and in my writing, I was feeling pretty relaxed. In a Crass kind of way, everything seemed to be going just fine. The album was due for release later that year, we had a series of tours lined up, and we were confident that things revolutionary were going very nicely, thank you. And then, blam, Margaret Thatcher declared war on a tiny island on the other side of the globe that no one had ever heard of. Under the weight of the jingoistic clap-trap which ensued, the Peace Movement all but collapsed (which, of course, was part of Thatcher's strategy of the time). In celebration of the Evil Empire's return to the forefront of global arrogance, Thatcher ordered that we 'rejoice' and, whilst Union Jacks were raised and knickers dropped, young men were slaughtered in their hundreds.

By then we had just about finished *Christ – The Album*, but given the distinctly nasty change in the political atmosphere, it all seemed a little pointless. Eventually it was released to be received with even more than the usual amount of venom that we had come to expect from the music press. Meanwhile, as Britain became smothered with red, white and blue bile, through a silence you could have sliced with an Exocet, Crass responded with a volley of hastily produced records articulating an utter contempt for the whole sickening business: *Sheep Farming in the Falklands*, *How Does It Feel to Be the Mother of a Thousand Dead?*, *Gotcha*, *You're Already Dead* and *Yes Sir, I Will*. Each one of them was pretty much unlistenable, screaming with an intensity and rage rarely heard before on vinyl. The reaction was immediate. The media labelled us 'traitors', it became a dodgy business visiting the local pub, and the Director of Public Prosecutions was ordered to bodge together a case of Criminal Obscenity against us. On top of this, record sales dropped noticeably. Yes, even the so-called Punk Movement appeared to have buckled under the strain. From then on we realised that, essentially, it was going to be a downhill slide.

In a country which likes to pride itself on its right to freedom of speech, there are some things you just can't say and hope to get away with. In short, we'd burnt our bridges. We began to feel very much on our own. Two years later, in 1984, Crass disbanded, tired and jaded, but at least proud that for the seven long years that we'd been together we had managed to remain intact both as a collective and, generally speaking, as a consistent voice.

After all these years, it was strange to be reading *The Last of the Hippies* again. It made me realise how different things had felt pre-Falklands. It was as if in those days there was a real chance that the voices of dissent could at last win through, that we were genuinely going to force some kind of radical social change. There's a naive optimism within *The Last of the Hippies* which, although I still feel great affection for, rather saddens me. It seems that I placed so much hope on the positive effects of pacifism that it had become something akin to a faith. By 1990, when I wrote my autobiography, *Shibboleth: My Revolting*

Life, I was already questioning some of those conceits. Doubt had set in. My faith was on the wane.

Throughout my life of revolt, my support has constantly veered between out and out pacifism and militant activism. Crass caught me at a time when pacifism seemed to be the way forward. Just at the moment, in 2008, I've swung heavily in the opposite direction. For all the well-intentioned peaceful protests against the this's and that's of global oppression, it seems pretty clear to me that no one is listening. The New World Order is winning hands down. The madmen are on top. Yes, we can form our self-help groups, call pub meetings to discuss a Left which has ceased to exist, kid ourselves that we're living our lives outside the System, but meanwhile the politicians, militarists, mafias and multinational corporations simply get on with their agenda of global slavery.

I don't want to be a slave, in fact I'm not going to be one. Filth like Tony Blair sticks in my gullet. The memory of Thatcher haunts my soul, violates everything that I consider to be decent and worthwhile. Wish them dead? Yes, well at least silenced, lots of times, but I'm too fucking nice to do anything about it, in any case, where would I start? Of course it would be revengeful, but just how much are we expected to put up with psychically damaging bullshit like Blair's 'I know I was wrong but feel I was right' or Bush's 'God told me to do it'. The truth is, I'm tired of being nice, but don't really know how to be nasty. But for all that, I'm equally tired of reformist drivellings. Never mind global warming, what about global warning? Have we listened? Have we learnt? Okay, so just because pacifism hasn't really worked, does that give cause to dismiss it? Of course not, but how many deaths do we have to witness? Are the Palestinians going to win their righteous cause by chanting slogans beneath the shadow of Israeli oppression? How many Jews escaped the death-camps through peaceful protest? How come the Special Relationship forces in Iraq don't take a week off to demol-ish the hideous Israeli walls? How come the powers that be can so easily destroy three thousand innocent lives in the WTC Reichstag yet can't put a stop to the partitioning of Israel? Democracy and peace? Closer to home, are the peace walls of Belfast bringing peace or bottling up hos-tility? Paradox after paradox, layer upon layer of incom-prehensible, cynical jargon. There's a time bomb waiting to go off and everybody knows it. And who planted it? Look no further than Westminster or the White House. When are we going to accept that since 9/11 we are all terrorists? We've been given the badge of office, so why don't we wear it? When are we going to stop apologising? 'Look here, George, I'm frightfully sorry, but I don't really quite agree with you killing children in Baghdad blah, blah, blah, blah, blah.' Over two million protesters waving banners on the streets of London proved to be as good as invisible. But what if they'd turned nasty? Yes, pacifism might be able to get us onto the streets, but sure as hell it won't liberate them. Surely by now it is horribly evident that in any situation where there might be a real break-through the System will bring out the heavy squad with the guns (like rats, they're never far away). They've got the weapons and don't mind using them, whereas we've got scruples, and that's a problem.

Way back in the eighties I got very tired of seeing friends being knocked about by the forces of law and order and then dragged off to the courts simply for asking for a better world. I recall a CND rally at which a young punk was being given a hard time by the Old Bill. I'd had enough, so I rushed over and whacked one of them. In the brief confusion which ensued, I did a runner with the young punk close on my heels. I'm not particularly proud of my action, but nonetheless it was gloriously satisfying, and I'm not embarrassed to admit it. Fill the jails? What a stupid, self-defeating business that is. If we continue to place ourselves in the role of victim, victims we will continue to be. There's got to be better ways than that.

The Last of the Hippies was written just before the Falklands farce and well before the Miners' Strike. These were turning points. Prior to them it really did seem that peace might have a chance and that the generally pacifist approach being taken was the right one. As things got heavier, so Crass (or a least I) was forced to consider taking a harder line. Amongst other things less openly discussable, we became heavily involved in events like the Stop the City riots which in turn inspired Reclaim the Streets, the Road Protests and, later, the G8 protests. But even those seem tame now. With egotists like Bono and Geldof undermining any truly radical discourse and action, with the Left completely destroyed by its own identity crisis, and with desperately restrictive new anti-terrorist legislation making Britain into a large-scale prison camp, it's hard to know where to turn next. One thing's for certain, it ain't rock'n'roll.

An element that greatly embarrasses me about *The Last of the Hippies* is the belief I had at the time that rock'n'roll was some kind of revolutionary force. What a delusion. I now realise that rock'n'roll was just another act of cultural imperialism, an outright theft of black culture. Elvis ripped off gospel, while some time later Mick Jagger crapped all over the noble heritage of the blues. But hey, it was only rock'n'roll and didn't we all like it? So yes, let's face it, the Pistols were no more than the Spice Girls of their day, glitzy, cheap and, dare I say it, downright crass. The Clash came in at a close second as ABBA with attitude. The fanciful dream expressed in *The Last of the Hippies* that rock'n'roll could act as some kind of radical world-changing force was archetypal of a form of inverted racism that has ensured that blacks remain firmly in their place and that whites can enjoy the delusion that they're 'just doing it'. Jagger was never anything more than a faux Tina Turner selling black sexuality as a white trash commodity. Sixties liberalism created a convenient illusion for the middle classes who most subscribed to it while making no real change to those who suffered its essential complacency: blacks, women and the working classes. I should have known better, but in 1982 I didn't.

Several years back I attended a punk conference at Wolverhampton University for which academics from all over the world had been invited to present papers on the 'punk phenomenon', in other words to put it into little boxes and wrap it all up. I went along because I knew what was going to happen, and it did. Apart from one notable exception, there was not one mention of Crass, nor of the powerful cultural movement that it had inspired. Academically speaking (and my god there was enough of that), punk was presented as little more than safety pins, glue-sniffing and gob. The issue so studiously avoided by our learned friends was that if it hadn't been for the politicisation of punk by bands like Crass, the whole pathetic pantomime would have been forgotten long ago.

Punk as lauded by the media was no more than an extension of the already reprehensible history of rock'n'roll.

Ironically, what is today commonly referred to as the 'punk movement' was from the very start inspired by and active within the political arena, however, it is the commercially-driven, self-interested King's Road coterie who continue to hog the limelight. The movement fomented by Crass was one of the most powerful cultural forces in late twentieth century Britain, yet does it get a mention in the history books? Does it hell. True, we never toppled Government, but we did give it an extremely uncomfortable run for its money and, what's more, continue to do so. I don't suppose that Margaret Thatcher has entirely forgotten that glorious afternoon during Questions In The House when she was asked whether she had taken time off to listen to the questions posed in our Falklands War single, *How Does It Feel to Be the Mother of a Thousand Dead?*. She declined to answer, but her Secret Service agents stuck at it. Thirty years on and they're still on the other end of the phone-line and, ASBO to the end, so am I.

What the Wolverhampton conference proved to me was the wholly collusive nature of the relationship between corporate capitalism, politics, the media and academia. If history is to serve the interests of the dominant culture, in this case that of commodification, then its writers, most of whom inhabit the hallowed halls of Oxbridge, must toe the line, which isn't very difficult given that corporate capitalism finances most academic institutions. Is it any wonder, then, that what the media dismissively labelled as anarcho-punk, the politicians reviled as a threat to decent society, and the corporate capitalists saw as unprofitable filth should have been so diligently left out of the history books? Do I expect anything different? Of course not. I have spent a lifetime opposing the status quo so I can hardly expect them to be singing my praises. At the very best, the loathing is mutual.

But here's another angle on the crunch, and a poignant one at that. A major difference between *The Last of the Hippies* and what I later wrote in *Shibboleth* (and continue to believe) is the truth concerning Wally Hope's death. It was murder by the State. For some reason (of personal cowardice?) I chose to avoid the issue in *The Last of the Hippies*. Was I afraid of State reprisals? Did I doubt the clear evidence I had that it was murder? I simply don't know, but I do know that in *Shibboleth* I attempted to put the record straight. So, if you want to know more about Wally and his untimely death, read *Shibboleth*.

That said, apart from a few edits and small additions, the following version of *The Last of the Hippies* is as it was written in 1982, warts'n'all. An awful lot has happened since then, and bugger me if I haven't just lost my bus pass.

—PENNY RIMBAUD, JUNE 2008

In this cell that is ours, there is no pity, no sunrise on the cold plain that is our soul, no beckoning to a warm horizon.

All beauty eludes us and we wait.

On the third of September 1975, Phil Russell, alias Phil Hope, alias Wally Hope, alias Wally, choked to death on his own vomit. Blackberry, custard, bile, lodged finally and tragically in the windpipe. Blackberry, custard, bile, running from his gaping mouth onto the delicate patterns of the ornamental carpet.

> *'No answer is in itself an answer.'*
> —Oriental proverb

Wally died a frightened, weak and tired man. Six months earlier he had been determined, happy and exceptionally healthy. It had taken only that short time for Her Majesty's Government's Health Department to reduce Wally Hope to a hopeless, puke-covered corpse.

> *'The first dream that I remember is of myself holding the hand of an older man, looking over a beautiful and peaceful*

> *valley. Suddenly a fox broke cover followed*
> *by hounds and strong horses ridden by*
> *red-coated huntsmen. The man pointed*
> *into the valley and said, 'that, my son, is*
> *where you're heading.' I soon found that*
> *out. I am the fox!'*
>
> —Wally Hope, 1974

For me, Wally's death marked the end of an era. He died alongside the last grain of trust that I naively had had in the System: the last seeds of hope. Prior to that, I had felt that if I lived a life based on respect rather than abuse my example might be followed by those in authority. Of course it was a dream, but reality is based on a thousand dreams of the past. Was it so silly that I should want to add mine to the future?

> *'It became necessary to destroy the town*
> *to save it.'*
>
> —Twentieth century military logic

World War Two was neither lost nor won, it simply created a horrific emptiness. Within that emptiness there grew a desperation amongst the peoples of the world, a fear that civilisation had learnt nothing from the tragic lessons of the Nazi death-camps or the cruel truths of

Hiroshima and Nagasaki. It seemed that those in power were setting the planet on a course towards total destruction. The arms race was full-swing. The Cold War was running amuck. The Third World was starving, but the superpowers looked only to themselves.

In the horror of this new world, people turned to bizarre ways of calming their fears. To ignore is the greatest ignorance, but ignore became the keyword as individuals buried themselves in the banalities of mindless materialism. The Age of Consumerism had been born. If you couldn't find peace of mind, perhaps a Cadillac would do. If life had lost its meaning, perhaps a super-deluxe washing machine might give it back. The 'this is mine, mine, mine' ownership and security boom was underway. Buy, buy, buy. Possess. Insure. Protect. The TV world was upon us. Which one's real? This one? That one? Mind-numbing crap to numb crappy minds. Buy this, buy that. Who knows which is which or what is what? Who cares? Buy this. Buy that. Layers of disposable, plastic-wrapped garbage to hide the awful facts of life in a nuclear reality.

BUY THIS.
BUY THAT.

Meanwhile, governments turned to the business of developing nuclear arsenals, nuclear 'deterrents' we were told, and the vast majority of the population, blinded by consumer gewgaws and media junk, was happy to accept the lie. As long as everyone was having fun, no one would question the behaviour of those in power as they played with their nuclear time-bombs. But all the time the fuse burnt shorter.

However, if the majority is always happy to be blown along by the prevailing wind, there are also those who will stand against it. If the fifties saw the birth of consumerism, it also gave rise to two powerful oppositional forces: the Peace Movement and rock'n'roll. Both were in reaction to a world increasingly dominated by the grey men of war and their grey thoughts. Both, at least initially, rejected the empty glitter of consumerism. Both represented a revolution against the abnormal values of 'normal' society.

The Peace Movement in Britain was founded on the platform of the newly formed Campaign for Nuclear Disarmament, CND, who by the end of the fifties was able to call thousands of protesters onto the streets to make their voice heard. But a louder voice still could be listened to at that time on the portable-radios and wind-up gramophones of millions of homes: the harsh new voice of rock'n'roll.

Whereas the Peace Movement was predominantly middle-class, rock'n'roll knew no class barriers, and although it probably took The Beatles to finally bring together the various disillusioned parties, rock'n'roll, revolution, a desire for change and the Peace Movement have from the very start been as good as inseparable.

Regrettably, by the beginning of the sixties, CND had become an accepted and therefore contained part of the British way of life. Its shout of protest had been dulled by the voice of moderation. The aims of CND had become increasingly obscured by political opportunism. Leftist vultures heavily disguised as doves had moved in and it became clear that the Labour Party saw CND as little more than a rung in the ladder to power. In 1964, as the opposition party, they promised to do away with Polaris, the nuclear submarine force. A few months later, after election to power, they ordered four new submarines. The disguise wore thin. Michael Foot, at that time a CND committee member (but now leader of the Labour Party), when asked if he would vote for an anti-bomb Tory Party rather than a pro-bomb Socialist one, replied 'certainly not'. It acted as a bewildering testament to his desire for peace.

The present rebirth of interest in CND runs the risk of once again going up the well-worn political arsehole. Socialist power-seekers have already moved in on the hard-fought-for peace platform. Speeches at the two most recent Trafalgar Square rallies were directed more towards vote catching than peace making. When the issues weren't so fashionable, the leftist 'doves' were happy enough to be sharing peanuts with the rest of the pigeons in the square. Now they are promising to refuse to allow America to install cruise missiles in Britain. Is this just another vote catcher that they will back off from if they are elected into power? If it is allowed to do so, the Labour Party will sail CND right down the river and sink it without trace.

Nuclear disarmament and the wider issues of peace must not be allowed to become political soap-operas in which the power-hungry can play out their cynicism. Further to this, and quite apart from the obvious threat of political exploitation, a very real danger to the long-term existence of CND and its allies is the current interest being shown in it by the music business. All of a sudden, peace has become a saleable commodity, a trendy product, and established record labels, the music press and bands alike, who four years ago dismissed those who opposed war as 'boring old hippies', are now bending over backwards to be seen to be supporting the cause. The only cause that they're supporting is their own. It's good promotion, good sales, good business, and they'll bleed it dry as long as it's this year's thing. When it isn't, they'll drop it, as they did Rock Against Racism, like a ton of hot bricks.

If by the mid-sixties the power of protest had dwindled, the power of rock was showing no such faint heart. Rock'n'roll ruled, and no party conference was going to bring it down. Youth had found its voice and increasingly was demanding that it should be heard. Loud within that voice was one that screamed promises of a new world: new colours, new dimensions, new time, new space. Instant karma, and all at the drop of an acid tab.

> *'My advice to people today is as follows. If you take the game of life seriously, if you take your nervous system seriously, if you take your sense organs seriously, if you take the energy process seriously, you must turn on, tune in, and drop out.'*
> —Acid prophet Timothy Leary

Respectable society was shocked. Desperate parents backed off as their little darlings tripped over the ornamental carpets. Hysterical reports that LSD caused everything from heartburn to mass suicide appeared almost daily in the press. Sociologists invented the generation gap, and when the long-haired weirdo flashed a V-sign at them they got that all wrong as well, it was really a peace sign, but either way round it meant 'fuck off'. In the grey corner we had what was normal'n'nice, and in the rainbow corner we had sex'n'drugs'n'rock'n'roll, at least that's how the media wanted us to see it. It was at this time that the CND symbol was adopted as an emblem by the ever-growing legions of rock fans whose message of love and peace spread like a prairie-fire, worldwide. In its desperate need to label and thus contain anything that threatens to outdo its control, the media named this phenomenon 'Hippie', and the System, to which the media is number one tool in the fight against change, set about in its transparent but nonetheless effective way to discredit the new vision. Rock'n'roll was achieving something that had never been achieved before, it was proving the falsity of the socially created divisions of colour, class and creed. The barriers were coming down. It didn't matter who you were, where you were from, or what you did. If you dug it, you were cool.

Despite what followers of Oi or Marx might say, rock'n'roll cannot be pigeon-holed to fit into any specific political ideology. It is the collective voice of the people, all the people, not just a platform for working class mythology, left, right or centre. Rock'n'roll is about freedom, not slavery. It's about revolution of the heart and soul, not convolution of the mind. To say that punk is or should be 'working class' is to falsely remove it from the classless roots of the 'rock revolution' from which it grew. Punk is a voice of dissent, an all out attack on the whole System. It as much despises working class stereotypes as it does middle class ones.

> *'Punk attacked the barriers of colour, class*
> *and creed, but look at how it is right now,*
> *do you really think you're freed?'*
> —Penny Rimbaud/Crass

Oi has been promoted in the pages of the music press as the 'real punk', but whereas punk aims to destroy class barriers, Oi is blind enough to be conned into reinforcing them. Oi's spokesman, Garry Bushell, who in all probability has never done a day's manual work in his life, claims that 'only the working class can change society'. Presumably he realises that his privileged professional status as a journalist prevents him from being in a position to contribute to his own pet theory. His myopic idea of what 'working class' means is little more than a middle class fantasy about a type of person who, except in the form of Alf Garnett and Andy Capp, just doesn't exist. His unrealistic view of workers as cloth-capped, beer-swilling, fist-waving jokers is a complete insult to genuine working people.

Oi would have been harmless enough if its comic-book caricatures of the workers hadn't appealed so strongly to the elements which were inevitably drawn to its reactionary views—the so-called 'right-wing'. Rather than rejecting its new and possibly unwanted following, Oi appeared to revel in its image of being 'nasty Nazi muzac for the real men'. Defending the trail of blood and bruises that it left behind itself wherever it went, the 'new breed' claimed that 'they weren't advocating violence, they were just reflecting the way things are'. Despite repeated evidence of Oi-inspired violence, it became increasingly obvious that Oi the Bushell and Oi the Bands were either perfectly happy with the way things were, or totally incapable of controlling the monster that they'd created.

At a time when something could have been done to change the image, the *Strength Through Oi* album was released, but rather than making an effort to shift the right-wing emphasis, it deliberately promoted it. The less than attractive cover sported your average skinhead about to land his cherry-reds up someone's khyber. But that week the cherries also left their mark on an old age pensioner's face. No matter, you can't win 'em all. Inside the sleeve, Oi the Bushell wrote about 'the sea of crop-heads running riot, knife-blades flashing in the moonlight'. Well, it's poetry, ain't it? But that week the knife-blades also flashed into an Asian youth's stomach. No matter, accidents will happen, won't they? The greatest 'accident' of them all, Southall, finally exposed Oi for the dangerous farce that it was. An Oi gig in a predominantly Asian community was inevitably going to cause problems. It would be unfair to suggest that the violence was deliberately planned by either the bands or the organisers of the gig, but given the reputation of Oi's following it should have been more than obvious that there would be trouble. Nonetheless, Oi the panto blindly marched in and, as the shit hit the fan, Southall burned and our jolly jokers, shaken and bruised, retreated to the pages of the press to protest their innocence. 'Well, the Asians weren't there for the concert, they only live there, don't they?' This time round, no one as much as giggled.

LEFT WING? RIGHT WING? YOU CAN STUFF THE LOT.

By the late sixties, straight society was beginning to feel threatened by what its youth was up to. It didn't want its grey towns painted rainbow. The psychedelic revolution was looking a little bit too real. It had to be stopped.

Books were banned and bookshops were closed down. Offices and social centres were broken into and their files were removed to be fed into police computers. Underground papers and magazines collapsed under the weight of official pressure. Galleries and cinemas had whole shows confiscated. Artists, writers, musicians and countless unidentified hippies were dragged through the courts to answer trumped-up charges of corruption, obscenity, drug abuse, or anything else that might silence their voice. But nothing could. It all mattered too much. As oppression became increasingly heavy, public servant 'bobby' became known as public enemy 'piggy'. War had been declared on the Peace Generation, but love wasn't going to give in without a fight.

And Charles said 'let there be death', and there was death, and the media and its faithful followers recoiled in horror at the thought that it might have been their child ordering the slaughter.

'Anything you see in me is in you. If you want to see a vicious killer, that's who you'll see. If you want to see me as your brother, that's who I'll be. It all depends on how much love you have. I am you, and when you can admit that, you will be free.'

—Charles Manson

Charles Manson, weaver of words, psychedelic warlord, witch-doctor of religious perversion, high-priest of fascist sexuality, hit back at the society that had distorted his vision with the distorted methods that society itself employs and teaches its young: violence.

And God so loved the world that he gave his only begotten son, Charles Manson. 'Piggy' written in blood on the polished surfaces of social acceptance.

'No more shall ye walk alone.'

Manson, his 'family', and the macabre killings for which they were responsible, sent shock waves through a smug and complacent society. Manson regarded the 'élite' of his Californian homeland as filth. These respectable people to whom he supplied drugs and from whom he often as not received no payment, were, to him, cheats and liars. These decent folk who wife-swapped, thrilled to video recordings of their illicit sexual conquests, revelled in snuff-movies, who saw flesh as something to be devoured, were, to him, barbarians. These pillars of society to whom organisations like the Mafia were a hidden support in their rise to grace, to whom the mysterious death of an opponent caused little more than a knowing lift of an eyebrow, were, to him, the enemy.

FILTH!

Manson's activities, extreme as they might have been, did represent a revolutionary stance, but because he had acted from a personal standpoint he was condemned by leftists who happily defended equally extremist groups like Baader-Meinhof or the IRA on the grounds that their position was political. This kind of double standard is the inevitable product of a society that sees its own boy soldiers as heroes and those of the enemy as murdering bastards, to whom its own massacres are victories and those of the enemy are massacres. Questions about the morality of violence are self-defeating. There is, and can be, no morality in violence. The vicious circle of violence rolls on and on. It can only be stopped by our refusal to be in any way a part of it.

Charles Manson made the mistake of setting out to destroy his enemy in the way that he believed they would destroy him: violence. But in some respects he was right. Hippies got along fine as long as they accepted that they were third-class citizens who should not expect anything but the garbage of consumer society. They were fine as long as they were prepared to live in shit and be treated like shit. When they ceased to do so, they came up against the whole weight of a society that had no place for the third-class citizens that it had created, they came up against the State violence which, euphemistically, is called 'law'.

> **Manson:** 'Do you really know where we are?'
> **Leary:** 'Where are we?'
> **Manson:** 'This is eternity brother. This is the end of the line. No one ever gets out once they've been here. This is for ever.'
> —Manson and Leary meet in jail

The Manson killings gave the media precisely what it was looking for. Hippies were suddenly no longer a passive, bead-wearing joke. They were potential psychopaths who, at the drop of a Beatles record, would knife their way to eternity. Forgetting that Hippie was a rejection of a society which governs with fear, controls by force and in the name of God has slaughtered millions of innocent victims, upright citizens waggled their trigger fingers at youth, saying, 'See, I told you so. That's what sex and drugs and rock and roll lead to'. They're still at it.

Ten years later, the same kind of media treatment was doled out to Sid Vicious. Despite attempts to silence it, punk had earned itself a voice and had become a household reality. However, the media was determined to undermine it. Nancy's sad death in a New York hotel brought out the same dull voices of self-righteous indignation as had the Manson killings. The trigger finger waggled again, and when Sid joined her in the great safety-pinned beyond, there was an almost universal chorus of 'see, I told you so'.

Manson and Sid were very different individuals with very different agendas, but their usefulness to the System was the same: identify the threat, select convenient scapegoats and use them to discredit the threat. Manson and Sid were both portrayed by the media as being typical of their kind, their actions being used to prove the misguided nature of all those of a similar appearance. The fact that their actions were as much condemned by their own kind as by anyone else was irrelevant to the media in its requirement to label, contain and destroy.

Each and every day, the TV, the radio and the newspapers manipulate and direct the thoughts of the general public, tell them what to think and how to think, but it's not because they want to improve the quality of thought, it's purely that they are required by the establishment interests that run them to reinforce 'standard' social values. Serve that which serves you, or else. When media is controlled almost exclusively by the wealthy ruling elite, censorship becomes unnecessary. Money speaks louder than words.

MURDOCH'S MONSTROUS MINIONS.

Manson's activities gave Hippie a new and, on the whole, unwanted dimension. Acid casualties became media satans, hippie cults became press devils, and both were subjected to a new wave of shock horror exposés. Acid was blamed for endless hideous crimes by the drunken, pill-popping power-mongers in authority, who, under heavy sedation from legally prescribed drugs, or reeling from the effects of excess alcohol, consider themselves fit enough to rule our world and qualified enough, should they consider it necessary, to destroy it. Hippie cults were attacked for doing precisely what established religion and psychology had been up to for centuries: mind fucking.

From Christ to Freud, there have always been those who, to compensate for their own personality defects, seek control and power by playing on the sense of loneliness and alienation of others. However, despite attempts to dismiss all hippies as dangerous psychopaths, the movement, although increasingly forced underground, grew both in numbers and in political awareness. Five years back, the message had been 'do your own thing' (exactly the message that fifteen years later Johnny Rotten was to repeat). The politics had been one of rejection. Society, the State and the System, had got nothing to offer. A whole generation had followed Leary's credo and dropped out.

> *'They formed little groups, like rich man's*
> *ghettoes, tending their goats and organic*
> *tomatoes. While the world was fucked by*
> *fascist regimes, they talked of windmills*
> *and psychedelic dreams.'*
> —Penny Rimbaud/Crass

Throughout this time, normal society, the State and the System, had benefited very nicely, thank you. They hadn't just stayed right where they were, they'd grown ever stronger. Slowly, as people woke up to the fact that turning on was turning off, and dropping out was copping out, the horrific reality of the nuclear world forced its way back through the escapist blur of those psychedelic dreams. The acid revolution had been fun, but that's just about where it had ended. Beneath the new space, the new time, the new dimensions and the new colours, the same old grey reality had ground relentlessly onwards. The dream was over. The dream had been that if you created your own life, independent of the System, the System would leave you to it. Looking back on it now, it seems pathetically naive, but for maybe fifteen years it had sustained the lives of thousands of people. The ultimate failure of Hippie was its ostrich-like approach to life. A hippie utopia surrounded by a world of hate and war was like 'snow before the summer's sun'. Eventually, those who weren't too permanently stoned to guarantee pipedreams to infinity, pulled their heads from the sands to confront a society that had got on very well without them for far too long. What was left of the Hippie Movement was finding a truly militant front for itself. Meanwhile, the Peace Movement had been all but destroyed by political greed and academic backbiting. The writing was on the wall. Things were going to have to change. This time round, peace was going to be a way of life, and love was going to rule supreme. And what's more, this time we'd be prepared to fight for it.

'We are a generation of obscenities. The most oppressed people in this country are not the blacks, not the poor, but the middle class. They don't have anything to rise up against and fight against. We will have to invent new laws to break. . . . The first part of the Yippie program is to kill your parents. . . . Until you're prepared to kill your parents, you're not ready to change this country. Our parents are our first oppressors.'
—Jerry Rubin, leader of the Yippies (militant hippies), speaking at Kent State University, USA

Within a month of Rubin's speech, the university was in uproar. The mostly white, middle class students had staged innumerable demonstrations and burnt down part of the university to show their objection to the way in which both their campus and their country were being run. The authorities called in the army to 'restore peace', which they did in true military fashion by shooting dead four students.

'After the shooting stopped, I heard screams and turned and saw a guy kneeling holding a girl's head in his hands. The guy was

getting hysterical, crying, yelling, shouting
"those fucking pigs, they shot you".
—A Kent State student

Although past history should have been a lesson to him, what Rubin hadn't accounted for was that parents would be prepared to kill their own children rather than accept change.

Mother: 'Anyone who appears on the streets of a city like Kent with long hair, dirty clothes or barefooted deserves to be shot.' Question: 'Is long hair a justification for shooting someone?' Mother: 'Yes. We have got to clean up this nation, and we'll start with the long-hairs.' Question: 'Would you permit one of your sons to be shot simply because he went barefooted?' Mother: 'Yes.'
—A mother speaks out

THE DAYS OF FLOWER POWER WERE OVER.

THE PIGGIES WERE OUT GRAZING IN THE MEADOWS.

'I'm very proud to be called a pig. It stands for pride, integrity and guts.'
—Ronald Reagan

By the end of the sixties, throughout the Western World, the people had returned to the streets. The dream was cross-fading with a social nightmare. In France, the Government was almost overthrown by anarchist students. In Holland, the Provos made a laughing stock of conventional politics. In Germany, Baader-Meinhof revenged itself on a State still run by ageing Nazis. In America, peace became a fierce battleground against war. In Northern Ireland, the Catholics rose up in demand for civil rights. In England, colleges and universities were occupied and embassies were stormed. People everywhere were calling for a life without fear, a world without war. They were demanding a freedom from the authorities who for years they had dismissed as almost nonexistent. The System, for far too long, had had it all its own way. However, amongst the people themselves a long standing animosity was becoming evident: the conflicting interests of anarchism and socialism.

From the mid-nineteenth century when Marx first forwarded his ideas, anarchists and socialists have clashed, sometimes violently, over their very different definitions of freedom. At the beginning of the twentieth century, following the Russian Revolution which anarchists had done much both to bring about and to win, the socialists with whom they had joined forces not only prevented them from playing a part in the new State, but actively and violently silenced them. In the thirties, anarchists and socialists fought against each other during the Spanish Revolution in which they had supposedly joined forces to oppose fascism. In the late sixties, French anarchists were in a position, given the support of the socialist unions, to overthrow the Government, but the unions backed off and the revolt collapsed. In countless other less grand scenarios the pattern has been repeated.

Anarchists reject Marxist concepts as 'dictatorship by the working class' which they see as being no better than 'dictatorship by the ruling class'. To the anarchist, all government and any government is oppression regardless of who is in control of it.

> *'The anarchist revolution that we want transcends the interests of a single class; it envisages the liberation of all humanity which is at present enslaved, either economically, politically, or morally.'*
> —Errico Malatesta

Anarchists believe that it is the right of individuals to make their own decisions in life, and that absolute free choice is essential to any real freedom. They reject all forms of government on the grounds that a governed society is a society in chains. It is inevitable that socialist ideas of organisation and centralisation should cause friction, since both are a form of control, and control, to an anarchist, is slavery. Socialism, like its supposed enemy, capitalism, is just another face to an age-old character: greed.

Ideological disagreements aside, the movement for change in the late sixties continued unabashed. Anarchist, socialist, activist, pacifist, working class, middle class, black, white, one thing united them all, a common cause, a universal factor, a shared flag: good old rock'n'roll. It was at that time that Woodstock in America and the Isle of Wight in Britain created a tradition in rock music that has now become part of our way of life: the music festival. Free music, free space, free mind; at least that, like 'once upon a time', is how the fairy story goes. The truth is there was one thing that certainly wasn't free: the entrance fee.

Many of the clashes between the authorities and the youth movement in the late sixties and early seventies were, broadly speaking, of a political nature, leftist platforms for social discontent, rather than anarchic demands by individuals for the right to live their own lives. Increasingly, anarchists sought the right to be able to celebrate their ideas away from both leftist propaganda and capitalist exploitation. It was from this desire that the concept of Free Festivals was born. The free festivals were to become an anarchist expression of freedom, as opposed to socialist demonstrations against oppression or capitalist opportunities for exploitation. As such, they presented the authorities with a new problem. How do you stop people having fun? The answer was horribly predictable. Stamp on them.

Windsor Park is one of Her Majesty's many back-gardens, and when the hippies rather foolishly decided that it was an ideal site for a free festival, she was not amused. Notwithstanding, the first Windsor Free was a reasonably quiet affair and the authorities had kept a low profile. Next year things were very different. The Queen's unwanted guests were forcibly removed by the police, and the royal corgis were, no doubt, suitably relieved. At the front of the clashing forces that year, dressed variously in nothing or a pair of faded jeans and a brightly embroidered shirt emblazoned with the simple message 'Hope', was Phil Russell, aka Wally Hope. He danced amongst the rows of police asking 'what kind of gentlemen are you?' or mocking 'what kind and gentle men you are.' The boys in blue were in fact men, and they were neither kind nor gentle. Wally came away from Windsor disturbed. He loathed violence and was sickened by what he had seen. Love? Peace? Hope? It was shortly after this that we first met.

For many years I had been running an open house. I was fortunate enough to have found a large country house at a very low rent, and felt that I wanted to share my luck. I had wanted to create a place where people could get together to work and live in a creative atmosphere rather than the stifling, inward looking family environments in which most of us had been brought up. Within weeks of opening the doors, people started turning up out of nowhere. Pretty soon we were a functioning community. It was inevitable, then, that someone like Wally would eventually pass our way.

Wally was a smiling, bronzed, hippie warrior. His eyes were the colour of the blue skies that he loved. His neatly cut hair was the gold of the sun that he worshipped. He was proud and upright, anarchistic and wild, pensive and poetic. His ideas were a strange mixture of the thinking of the peoples whom he admired and amongst whom he had lived. The dancing Arabs. The peasant Cypriots. The noble Masai. The silent and sad North American Indians, for whom he felt a particular closeness of spirit.

The North American Indians regarded the land upon which they lived in much the way that we regard the air that we breathe, as something that could not be owned. How could anyone claim to have ownership of something that constantly grows and changes? However, in their greed for land, white settlers made exactly those claims, and the Native Indians were quickly and savagely reduced to nothing more than prisoners in the concentration camps that the American Government laughingly call 'reservations'.

> *'The earth was created by the assistance of the sun and it should be left as it was. The country was made without barriers and it is no man's business to divide it. I see the whites all over the country gaining wealth, and see their desire to give us lands which are worthless. The earth and myself are of one mind. The measure of the land and the measure of our bodies are the same.'*
> —An American Indian describes his feelings for land

Oppression of what remains of the American Indian peoples continues to this day. They are forced to live at the arse-end of a society that has grown rich on the exploitation of their lands. Areas that at one time the US Government considered worthless and therefore suitable for reservations, are, in the event of valuable minerals being found on them, forcibly reclaimed. Meanwhile, the native peoples are resettled on still more worthless ground. A whole race of people have been made homeless in their own homeland.

> *'Yes, we know that when you come, we die.'*
> —An American Indian describes
> his feelings for white men

Wally had travelled the world and had met fellow-thinkers in every place that he had stopped, but always he returned to England. Perhaps it was his love of the mythical past, King Arthur and His Knights, that brought him back, or perhaps he felt as I do, that real change can only be effected in the place that you most understand: home.

Wally could talk and talk and talk. Half of what he spoke about seemed like pure fantasy, the other half like pure poetry. He was gifted with a strange kind of magic. One day in our garden, it was early summer, he conjured up a snowstorm, huge white flakes settling amongst the daisies on the lawn. Another time he created a multi-rainbow sky. It was as if he had cut up a rainbow and thrown the pieces into the air where they hung in strange random patterns. On reflection it seems unbelievable, but, all the same, I can remember both occasions vividly.

On our first meeting, Wally described Windsor Free and other gatherings that he had attended. Not particularly liking crowds, I had always chosen to avoid festivals, so my knowledge of them was very limited. Wally outlined their history and then went on to detail his ideas for the golden future. He proceeded to unfold what seemed to me to be a ludicrous plan. He wanted to claim back Stonehenge, a place that he regarded as sacred to the people and stolen by the Government. He wanted to make it into a site for free festivals: free music, free space, free mind. At least that, like 'happily ever after', is how the fairy story goes.

It is sad that none of that freedom was evident ten years later when Crass, the band of which I was a founder member, attempted to play at the Stonehenge Free Festival. Since Wally's death, it had been a dream that one day I might play the festival as a kind of memorial to him. In 1980 I had the band and the opportunity to do it. By then

Crass was enjoying quite a degree of notoriety, and our presence at Stonehenge attracted several hundred punks to whom the festival scene was a novelty. They, in turn, attracted interest from various factions to whom punk was equally new. Initially the atmosphere seemed relaxed and, as dusk fell, thousands of people gathered around the stage to listen to the night's music. Suddenly, for no apparent reason, a group of bikers stormed the stage saying that they were not going to tolerate punks at 'their festival'. What followed was one of the most violent and frightening experiences of my life. Bikers armed with bottles, chains and clubs stalked around the site viciously attacking any punk they set eyes on. There was nowhere to hide, nowhere to escape to. All through the night we attempted to protect ourselves and other terrified punks from this mindless violence. There were screams of terror as people were dragged off into the darkness to be given lessons in peace and love. It was hopeless trying to save anyone because in the blackness of night they were almost impossible to find. Meanwhile, the predominantly hippie gathering, lost in the soft blur of a stoned reality, remained oblivious to our fate.

Weeks later, a hippie news-sheet defended the bikers, saying that they were an anarchist group who had misunderstood our motives. Some misunderstanding! Some anarchists!

If Wally and the first Stonehenge festivals were my first flirtations with real hippie culture, this was probably my last.

Burnt-out hippies were a common phenomenon in the early seventies, lost souls whose brains were governed more by dope and acid than by common-sense. They were generally a bore, waffling on about how things were 'going to be' whilst making no effort whatsoever to work towards that end or, indeed, any end whatsoever. For all his strange ideas, Wally seemed different. To him, drugs were not something to drop out with, but a communion with a reality of colour and hope which he actively brought back into the world of greyness and despair. He used drugs carefully and creatively, not for escape, but to help realise a means of escape.

In many respect I could never have been described as a hippie. After the usual small amount of experimentation, I had rejected the use of drugs because I found that they confused my thoughts and interfered with my relationships. Equally, the house that I had set up had never been designed to act as a place where people could 'drop out'. I wanted somewhere where people could 'drop in' and realise that, given their own time and space, they could actively create their own sense of purpose and, most importantly, their own lives. I wanted to offer a place where people could be something that the System never allows them to be: themselves. In many respects this was closer to anarchist traditions than to hippie ones, but, inevitably, there was an interaction.

I had opened up the house to all-comers at a time when many others were doing the same. The so-called 'Commune Movement' was the natural result of people like myself wishing to create lives of cooperation, understanding and sharing. Individual housing is one of the most obvious causes for the desperate shortage of homes. Communal living is a practical solution to the problem. If we could learn to share our homes, maybe we could learn to share our world. That is the first step towards a state of sanity.

I shared Wally's disgust with straight society, a society that puts more value on property than on people, that respects wealth more than it does wisdom. I supported his vision of a world where the people took back from the State what the State had stolen from the people. In that sense, squatting is every bit as much a political statement as it is a personal solution. Why should we have to pay for what is rightfully ours? Whose world is this? Maybe squatting Stonehenge wasn't such a bad idea after all.

The lives of millions upon millions of people are run by a small handful of ruling elites who own all the wealth, all the land, and who have all the control. We are expected to be grateful to them for the privilege of having them rule our lives. We are expected to be grateful to them for the privilege of paying them for the roof over our heads. We are expected to be grateful to them for the privilege of being slaves in their factories and offices and for the privilege of accepting the miserable wages that they so resentfully dole out to us. We are expected to be grateful for the privilege of paying them their huge taxes so that they can further finance their oppression of us, the people. They grow richer at our expense, but we are expected to look up to them as examples of success. Finally, we are expected to be grateful to them for the privilege of fighting for them in their wars and killing other people like ourselves, or being killed by other people like ourselves. We are expected to love, honour and obey this wife-beater 'til death, quite probably premature, do us part. In this particular marriage, divorce is a hard case to fight for.

> *'Do they owe us a living? Of course they fucking do!'*
>
> —Steve Ignorant/Crass

Wally kept coming back to the house with new plans. His enthusiasm was infectious and finally he was able to persuade me and my fellow residents to join the cause. We agreed to help him organise the first Stonehenge Festival, Summer Solstice, June 1974.

> *'Then called King Arthur with loud voice,*
> *"where here before us the heathen hound,*
> *who slew our ancestors, now march we to*
> *them ... and when we come to them, myself*
> *foremost of all the fight I will begin".*
> —'Brut' Layamon

By the beginning of 1974 we had printed thousands of handouts and posters and had sent out hundreds of invitations to such varied celebrities as the Pope, the Duke of Edinburgh, The Beatles, the British Airways air hostesses and the Hippies of Kathmandu. Needless to say, not many of the invitees turned up on the appointed date, but Wally was happy enough with the motley crew of a few hundred hippies who did.

For nine weeks, Wally and those who were prepared to brave the increasingly wet summer held fort at the old stone monument, watched in growing confusion by the old stone-faced monument keepers. Wood-smoke curled into the damp night air, grey smoke against grey stones. Leaping flames illuminated the storytellers who sat, rainbow splashes in the plain landscape, telling tales of how it was that this fire came to be lit in this place, at this time, here on our earth.

> *'Our generation is the best mass movement in history, experimenting with anything in our search for love and peace. Knowledge, kicks, religion, life, truth. Even if it leads us to our death, at least we're all trying, together. Our temple is sound. We fight our battles with music, drums like thunder, cymbals like lightning, banks of electronic equipment like nuclear missiles of sound. We have guitars instead of tommy-guns.'*
> —Phil Russell, 1974

'Even if it leads us to our death . . .'

Rock'n'roll'n'revolution, day in, day out. The talk went on, the rain came down and, if this year there'd only been a battered old cassette-player to pump out the sounds, next year they'd do better.

Eventually, the Department of the Environment, keepers of the old stone-faced monument keepers, served the 'Wallies of Stonehenge' notice to withdraw from Government property. The various inhabitants of the fort had agreed that should the authorities intervene they would answer only to the name of Wally, the name originating from a dog lost at the Isle of Wight Festival of many years back, when thousands of rock fans chanted 'Wally, Wally, Wally,' well into the night until the poor mutt was found. Equally ludicrous were the surreal summonses served against Phil Wally, Sid Wally, Chris Wally, Starburst Wally, Willy Wally and all the rest of the motley crew of Wallies. It was a case of Wally here, Wally there, Wally almost everywhere, and it did much to set the scene for the absurd trial that followed in London's High Courts.

Fleet Street loved it. Of late there hadn't been any suitably unpleasant murders, rapes, wars or natural disasters with which to amuse readers, so the Wallies, with their leader, Wally Hope, became this week's disposable stars. The grinning heroes appeared daily in the pages of the press, flashing peace-signs and preaching the power of love next to that day's tits'n'bums. It was an old message in a new setting.

Having lost the case and been ordered to immediately vacate the land, Wally jubilantly left the courtroom to face waiting reporters announcing, 'We have won, we have won. Everybody loves us. We have won.' Win or lose, everybody was certainly confused by Wally's somewhat disposable statement. All the same, for a day or two the Wallies had been good copy, and in some respects they had won. They had moved on, but there was always next year to think about. A tradition had been born, a tradition which was to become legendary within the history of free festivals. But Wally Hope had pushed a thorn into the side of the System, and the System wasn't going to let him get away with it again.

From Stonehenge the retreating Wallies moved to Windsor. This year the festival had attracted the biggest gathering ever. Tens of thousands of people had come to ensure that Her Royal Majesty remained unamused and she, in turn, was waiting in the guise of a massive police presence. Tension between the two factions existed from the very start, and eventually things exploded when the police staged a vicious early morning attack on the sleeping festival goers. Hundreds of people were injured as the police randomly and brutally laid into anyone unlucky enough to be in their way. People were dragged from their tents to be treated to a breakfast of boot and abuse. Protesting hippies were jostled away to waiting Black Marias to be insulted, intimidated, beaten up and charged. While revelling over every moment of it, the media pretended to be shocked, and the Government ordered a public enquiry, neither of which doing much to improve the condition of the hundreds of injured people.

Government enquiries are frequently used to trick the general public into thinking that something positive is being done about situations where the System has been seen to step out of line. These token gestures allow the authorities to commit atrocious crimes against the people while suffering no real fear of reprisal. The tactic has been employed in cases of military and police violations from Belfast to Brixton, in cases of environmental violations such as deadly radiation leaks from power stations like Windscale in Cumbria, and in compulsory purchase orders on land for motorways, airports and nuclear plants, all of which are more likely to be a part of Government plans for the event of nuclear war than to be for the convenience of the public. In short, the tactic is used whenever the Government needs to cover-up its activities, be it corruption by Government officials, the maltreatment of inmates in prisons and mental homes or violence by teachers in schools. Those in Government are perfectly aware that they and the authorities to whom they have given power, daily commit crimes against the public. Yet, unless they are exposed by that same public, who in doing so might rightly fear for their own well-being, nothing is done. In cases where the public do become aware of inexcusable behaviour by the authorities, the Government sets up its own enquiry to 'investigate' the issue. Something appears to be happening and the gullible, silent, violent majority are satisfied that justice has been done. However, the crude fact is that nothing at all will have been done apart from the production of a few White Papers that hardly anyone will read and no one will take any notice of. Meanwhile, the official crimes continue unhindered.

Wally Hope came away from Windsor bruised and depressed. Once again he had danced amongst the boys in blue in a vain attempt to calm them down with his humour and his love. He had been severely beaten up for his efforts.

> *'I saw the police dragging away a young boy, punching and kicking him. I saw a pregnant woman being kicked in the belly, and a little boy being punched in the face. All around the police were just laying into people. I went to one policeman who had just knocked out a woman's teeth and asked him why he'd done it. He told me to fuck off or I'd get the same. Later on I did.'*
>
> —Wally Hope, after the party was over

Bit by bit, we were learning. Our parents, at least their public servants, were our first oppressors. The daisies were being eaten by the beast. The nightmare was becoming a reality.

> *'Where today are the many powerful tribes of our people? They have vanished before the greed and oppression of the White Man as snow before the summer's sun.'*
> —American Indian Chief

In the winter of that year, Wally started work at our house on the second Stonehenge Festival: posters, hand-outs, invites. This time round he had the questionable success of the first festival to point to, so the job was easier. Word of mouth has always been a powerful tool of the underground and people were already talking about what they would do to make it work. Wally spent much of the first two months of '75 handing out leaflets in and around London. Dressed in his combat uniform, a bizarre mixture of middle-eastern army gear and Scottish tartans, and driving his rainbow-striped car complete with a full sized Indian tepee strapped to the roof, he was a noticeable and colourful sight, a sight that those greyer than himself both in appearance and thought would certainly not have missed.

I recall at the time feeling a deep sense of apprehension. Wally seemed just a little bit too confident, a little less inclined to check on important details, a little too ready to allow anyone on board. I had always believed that trust was an absolute fundamental, but I was beginning fear that Wally was giving just a little too much. But he was on a roller-coaster and who was I to be issuing warnings?

In May, he left our house for Cornwall. We had done all that we could to prepare for the festival, and Wally wanted to rest up in his tepee until it began. The day of his departure was brilliantly hot. We sat in the garden drinking tea as Wally, glorifying the golden sun, serenaded us and it with a suitably wild performance on his tribal drums. He was healthy, happy and confident that this time round he really would win. Later, as the rainbow-striped car drew away from our house, he leant through its window and let out an enormous shout, something in between an Indian war-cry and the words 'freedom and peace'. He was too far away to be properly heard. Later that day it rained.

The next time that we saw him, about a month later, he was as good as unrecognisable. He had lost a stone in weight and his skin was white and unpleasantly puffy. He was frail, nervous and almost incapable of speech. He sat with his head hung on his chest, his tongue running across his lips as if searching out the face to which it had once belonged. His tear-filled eyes had sunk, dull and dead, into his skull like some obscene Halloween mask. His hands shook constantly in the way that old men's do on a cold wintry day. The sun which he worshipped had darkened for him. He was unable to bear its light or its heat. Every so often he would take pained, involuntary glances around the walled garden in which we sat. Occasionally our eyes would follow his, and always they were met with other more sinister eyes watching us from across the perfect lines of the neatly cut green lawns. Wally Hope was a prisoner in one of Her Majesty's Psychiatric Hospitals. A man with no future but theirs. This time round he certainly was not winning.

A couple of days after Wally had left our house, he had been arrested for possession of three acid tablets. The police had mounted a raid on a squat where he had stopped for the night, claiming that they were looking for an army deserter. It just so happened that while they were looking for the deserter they decided to look through Wally's coat pocket. Of course they hadn't noticed the rainbow-striped car parked outside, nor were they aware of the fact that the owner of that coat was the laughing hippie anarchist who had made such a fool of the courts only a year before, or that he was the same colourful character who just a few days ago had been handing out festival leaflets on the streets of London. The police don't notice things like that. Their job, after all, is to catch fictitious army deserters.

Whereas most people would have been given a large waggle from the trigger-finger and a small fine, Wally was refused bail and kept in prison on remand. He was refused the use of the phone or of letter writing materials, so he had no way of letting people on the outside know what had happened to him. The people from the squat in which he was arrested did nothing to help, presumably because they feared similar treatment by the authorities. He was alone and hopelessly ill-equipped for what was going to happen to him.

After several days in jail, he appeared on parade wearing pyjamas, claiming that the prison clothing, which he was obliged to wear, was giving him rashes. Rather than suggesting the simple remedy of allowing him to wear his own clothes, the warder, clearly an expert in medical matters, sent him to see the prison doctor who in his infinite wisdom had no trouble at all in diagnosing the problem as 'schizophrenia'.

> *'Just because they say that you're paranoid, it doesn't mean that you're not being followed.'*
>
> —Unknown hippy wit

Since the beginning of time, mental illness has been used as a powerful political weapon against those seeking or operating social change. A lot of the bogus definitions given for so-called madness were invented in the twentieth century by quack psychologists and were then used unscrupulously by those in authority to dismiss and often punish those who dared to question their reality. In truth, terms like 'schizophrenia', 'neurotic' and 'paranoid' mean little more than what any particular, or not so particular, individual chooses them to mean. There are no physical proofs for any of these conditions. The definitions vary from psychiatrist to psychiatrist and are totally different from one country to another. Because of these very variable standards, the chances of being diagnosed schizophrenic in America are far higher than they are in Britain. This led one unusually illuminated psychiatrist to suggest that the best cure for many American mental patients would be to catch a flight to Britain. The label of mental illness is a method of dealing with individuals, from unwanted relatives to social critics who, through not accepting the conditions imposed upon them by outsiders, are seen as nuisances and trouble makers.

The works of psychologists, notably Freud, and the many schools of perverts who follow their teachings, have, by isolating 'states of mind' and defining some of them as 'states of madness', excluded all sorts of possible developments in the way in which we see, or could see, our reality. By allowing people to learn from the experience of their so-called madness rather than punishing them for it, new radical ways of thought could be realised and engaged with, new perspectives created and new horizons reached. How else has the human mind grown and developed? Nearly all the major advances in society have been made by people who are criticised, ridiculed and often punished in their own time, only to be celebrated as great thinkers years after their deaths. As mental and physical health becomes increasingly controllable with drugs and surgery, we come ever closer to a world of hacked about and chemically processed Mr. and Mrs. Normals whose only purpose in life will be to mindlessly serve the System. From then on, cultural progress will cease and the mind-fuckers will finally have won their battle against the human spirit.

DEMOCRACY?

LET'S CALL IT BRAINWASHING.

Once labelled 'mad', a patient may be subjected to a whole range of hideous tortures politely referred to by The National Health Service as cures. They are bound up in belts, harnesses and strait-jackets so that their bodies become bruised and their spirits beaten. They are locked up in silent padded-cells so that the sound of their own heartbeat and the smell of their own shit breaks them down into passive animals. They are forced to take psychotropic drugs that make them into robot-like zombies. One common side-effect of long-term treatment with these drugs is severe swelling of the tongue. The only effective cure is surgical. The tongue is cut out. What better way to silence the prophet? They are given electric shocks in the head that cause disorientation and loss of memory. ECT, electroconvulsive therapy, is an idea adopted from the slaughterhouse where pigs are stunned with an identical form of treatment before having their throats cut. ECT is a primitive form of punishment that owes more to the traditions of the witch hunts than it does to any tradition of science. The ultimate cure, the tour de force of the psychiatric profession, is lobotomy. Victims of this vile practical joke have knives stuck into their heads that are randomly waggled about so that part of the brain is reduced to mincemeat. The surgeons who perform this operation have no precise idea what they are doing. The brain is an incredibly delicate organ about which very little is known, yet these butchers feel qualified to poke knives into people's heads in the belief that they are performing scientific and medical services. Patients who are given this treatment frequently die from it. With rare exceptions, those who don't die can never hope to recover from the state of mindlessness that has been deliberately imposed upon them.

Disgusting experiments are daily performed both on animals and humans in the name of medical advance. There is no way of telling what horrific new forms of treatment are at this moment being devised for us in the thousands of laboratories throughout the country. In Nazi Germany, the inmates of the death camps were used by drug companies as guinea pigs for new products. Nowadays the drug companies, some of which are the very same ones, use prisoners in jails and hospitals for the same purposes. Mental patients are constantly subjected to the ignorance both of the State and the general public and, as such, are perhaps the most oppressed people in the world. In every society there are thousands upon thousands of people locked away in asylums for doing nothing more than question imposed values, dissidents dismissed by the label of madness and silenced, often for ever, by the cure.

Wally was prescribed massive doses of a drug called Largactil which he was physically and often violently forced to take. Drugs like Largactil are widely used not only in mental hospitals, but also in jails where their use is not officially permitted. Wally had found this out to his cost; the prison doctor's treatment for schizophrenia had quickly reduced him to a state of helplessness. By the time he was dragged into the courts to face charges he was so physically and mentally bound-up in a drug-induced strait-jacket that he was totally incapable of understanding what was going on, let alone of offering any kind of defence for himself.

When at last we did hear from him, an almost incomprehensible letter that looked as if it had been written by a five year old child, he had been taken from the jail, herded through the courts where he had been sectioned under the Mental Health Act of 1959, and committed, for an indefinite period, to a mental hospital.

Sectioning, which in truth is no more than compulsory hospitalisation, is a method by which the authorities can imprison anyone who two doctors are prepared to diagnose as mad. Naturally, it is not difficult to find willing doctors. Prison hospitals are riddled with dangerous hacks who, having sunk to the bottom of their profession, are all too willing to oblige. Once sectioned, the patient loses all normal human rights, can be treated in any way that the doctors see fit and, because appeal against the court decision is almost impossible, stands no chance of release until certified cured by those same doctors. Sectioning enables the State to take anyone off the streets and imprison them, indefinitely, without any crime having been committed. It enables the State, within the letter of the law, to torture and maim prisoners and suffer no fear of exposure. Compulsory hospitalisation is the ultimate weapon of our oppressive State, a grim reminder of the lengths to which the System will go to control the individual. Whereas the bomb is a communal threat, sectioning violates the very principle of individual human rights in its direct threat to the freedom of personal thought and action. Britain was recently forced by the European Court of Human Rights to allow its citizens the right to appeal against compulsory hospitalisation. Although this might appear to be an improvement on what existed in Wally's time, patients still have to wait at least six months before the appeal will be heard, by which time, like Wally, they are liable to be so incapacitated by the treatment they have received that the appeal procedure would be impossible for them to handle.

When we heard of Wally's fate, we were convinced that the experience would destroy him. Some of us, including myself, were convinced that the authorities intended to destroy him. Inevitably, we were assured by liberal acquaintances that we were just being paranoid, but those same liberals said the same about any of the horrors of modern technological society, from the bombs to computer systems, that they were afraid to confront within themselves. Paranoid or not, we made efforts, firstly legally, then illegally, to secure Wally's release. All of our attempts failed.

We spent days on the phone contacting people whom we thought might be able to help or advise us. The most useful and compassionate help came from organisations like Release and BIT, underground groups, some of which still operate today, helping people on all sorts of problems from housing to arrest.

We soon realised that an appeal would be as good as impossible and, in any case, to follow legal procedures could take months and by then it would be too late. We employed a lawyer to act on Wally's behalf, but the hospital made it impossible for him to contact Wally. Letters never got through. Telephone calls proved pointless. The patient was always resting. We then attempted to visit Wally in hospital, but were informed that no one but his close relatives could see him. His father had died and his mother and sister, neither of whom would have anything to do with him, were abroad. Gambling on the chance that the staff knew little about his family background, one of us, posing as his sister, finally gained access to the hospital. Quite apart from simply wanting to see Wally, the aim of the visit was to plan a means of kidnapping him so that he could be taken away somewhere to recover from his ordeal.

On a second visit, I was able to accompany 'Wally's sister' without arousing suspicion. We had hoped to finalise the kidnap plan, but we found him in such bad health that we realised it could be damaging to him to have to deal with the kind of movements we had planned. What neither of us realised at the time was that, rather than being the symptoms of mental illness, his appalling condition was the direct result of the treatment that he was being given.

The sad, shuffling half-people that can be seen through the railings of any mental hospital are like that not because of the illness that they supposedly have, but because of the cures that they are being subjected to. The social stereotype of the grey raincoated loony is a tasteless twist more worthy of a B movie than of any civilised society, it is one which is forced either surgically or chemically onto the patient whose moronic and lifeless appearance is then used as proof of their supposed illness.

Since his admission into hospital, Wally had been receiving pills to cure his schizophrenia, and injections to counteract the side effects of the pills. Naturally, he had been slipping the pills under his tongue and spitting them out later. The injections were unavoidable. The hospital nurses were mostly male and considerably stronger than him, so polite refusals were of little use, but in any case it didn't really matter because the injections were being given to counteract the side-effects of the pills that he wasn't taking. What neither he nor we knew was that the hospital staff had deliberately lied to him about which medicine was which. The result was that the injections, of a drug called Modecate of which he was receiving doses massively above those recommended by the manufacturers, were creating increasingly serious side-effects that were not being treated. It should have been obvious to the staff that something was going amiss. They must have realised that Wally was spitting out the pills, but that, after all, was part of their cure. He was systematically and brutally being made into a mindless moron.

Meanwhile, the second Stonehenge Festival took place. This year thousands of people turned up, and for over two weeks the authorities were unable to stop the festivities. Wood-fires, tents and tepees, free food stalls, stages and bands, music and magic. Flags flew and kites soared. Naked children played in the woodlands, miniature Robin Hoods celebrating their material poverty. Dogs formed woofing packs that excitedly stole sticks from the innumerable wood piles and then scrapped over them in tumbling, rolling bundles of fur. Two gentle horses were tethered to a tree and silently watched the festivities through the dappled light that danced across their bodies. Old bearded men squatted on tree stumps muttering prayers to their personal gods. Small groups of people tended puffing fires upon which saucepans bubbled and bread baked, the many rich smells blending across the warm air. Parties of muscular people set out in search of wood and water accompanied always by a line of laughing, mimicking children.

Everywhere there was singing and dancing. Indian flutes wove strange patterns of sound around the ever-present bird song. The beat of drums echoed the hollow thud of axe on wood. Old friends met new, hands touched, bodies entwined, minds expanded and, in one tiny spot on our earth, love and peace had become a reality.

Just ten miles down the road, Wally Hope, the man whose vision and hard work had made this reality possible, was being pumped full of poisons in the darkness of a hospital cell.

THE EXECUTION OF HOPE

A couple of days after the last person had left the festival site, without any prior notice, Wally was set free. The grey men had kept the smiling, bronzed, hippie warrior from his festival and now, having effected their cure, ejected a nervous gibbering wreck onto their grey streets. It took Wally two days to drive his rainbow-striped car from the hospital to our home. Seventy miles in two days. Two days of terror. He found himself incapable of driving for any length of time and had to stop for hours on end to regain his confidence. No one knew of his release and, maybe to restore some kind of dignity for himself, he was determined to do it alone. When he finally arrived at our house he was in an even worse condition than when we had seen him at the hospital. He was barely able to walk, and even the most simple of tasks was impossible for him. It is hard to believe that he was able to drive those seventy miles at all. This pale shadow of the person who we had once known now found it agony to sit in the sun. His face and hands would swell up into a distorted mess. The sun that he worshipped was now all darkness for him. At night he would lay in his bed crying quiet, desperate sobs that would go on until dawn, when finally he would go to sleep. Nothing seemed to help his pathetic condition. We tried to teach him to walk properly again, but he was unable to coordinate. His left arm would swing forward with his left leg, his right with his right. Sometimes we were able to laugh about it, but the laughter always gave way to tears. We couldn't understand and we were afraid. Finally, out of desperation we managed to get him to a doctor who diagnosed his condition as 'chronic dyskinesia', a disease brought about through overdoses of Modecate and related drugs. Wally had been made into a cabbage and worse, an incurable one.

Bit by bit, the realisation that he was doomed to live in a half-world of drug-induced idiocy made its way into what was left of his brain. On the third of September 1975, unable to face another day, perhaps hoping that death might offer more to him than what was left in life, Wally Hope overdosed on sleeping pills and choked to death on the vomit that they induced.

In the relatively short time that we have on this earth we probably have contact with thousands of people with whom we share little more than half-smiles and polite conversation. We are lucky if amongst those thousands of faces one actually responds to us with more than predictable formalities. Real friends are rare. True understanding between people is difficult to achieve, and when it is achieved it is the most precious of all human experiences. I have been lucky in that I am part of a group of people whom I regard as friends and with whom I can share a sense of reality and work towards a shared vision of the future. Equally, I have met a few people who because of their own cynicism and lack of purpose appear to want to prevent people like ourselves from expressing our own sense of our own lives. I see people like that as the dark shadows that have made our world so colourless.

Wally was a genius. I can't pretend to have completely liked him, he was far too demanding to be liked, but I did love him. He was one of the most colourful characters that I have ever met, a person who had a deep sense of destiny and no fear whatsoever in pursuing it. If friends are rare, people like Wally are very, very rare indeed. I don't suppose I shall ever meet someone quite like him again. He was a magical, mystical visionary who demonstrated more to me about the meaning of life than all the grey nobodies who have ever existed could ever hope to do. He was an individual, pure energy, a great big golden light that shone in the darkness, who because he was kind, gentle and loving, was seen by those grey people as a threat, a threat that they felt should be destroyed. Wally was not mad, not crazy, not a nutter. He was a human being who didn't want to have to accept the grey world that we are told is all we should expect in life. He wanted more and set out to get it. He didn't see why we should have to live as enemies to each other. He believed, as do most anarchists, that people are basically kind and good and that it is the restrictions and limitations forced upon us, often violently by uncaring Systems, that creates evil.

> *'What is evil but good tortured by its own hunger and thirst?'*
> —Phil Russell quoting The Prophet, 1974

We are born free, but almost immediately we are subjected to conditioning in preparation for a life of slavery within the System. We are moulded by our parents, teachers, preachers and bosses to conform to what they want from us rather than to our own natural and unique desires. Anarchists believe that those natural desires for peaceful and cooperative lives are denied us because they do not serve the requirements of the ruling classes. Life should and could be a wonderful and exciting experience. Despite what the politicians say, the world is big enough for us all if we could only learn to share it and to respect each other within it. Millions of people are governed by very few. Millions of lives of grey slavery simply so that those few can enjoy the privileges that are the birth right of us all. Surely, by sheer weight of numbers we have the strength to take back what is rightfully ours? But then we are faced with that age-old dilemma. Do we have the right to use violence to force our demands? The anarchist answer would have to be 'no'.

Armed revolution as advocated by extremists both of the Left and the Right is nothing more than destructive revenge, an unpleasant tactic learnt in the school playground and never forgotten. To say that violence is the only way to achieve improvements for the common good is to say that people are basically bad and unchangeable, an unacceptably cynical view that runs deep through most political thought. Those who advocate armed revolution are seeking to oppress those who they see as enemies in exactly the same way as those enemies oppressed them. The boot is simply placed on another foot. Force can only lead to resentment. If force is used to make someone do something against their will, they will eventually fight back. The same applies to armed revolution. If a revolution is won by violent means, it will inevitably create violent reaction. The vicious circle of violence rolls on and on, and nothing but the name of the oppressor will have changed. Anarchists believe that it is essential to break that circle of violence as it is precisely that which distorts and perverts people's basic kindness and goodness. Anarchists believe that it is the right of the individual to make their own decisions free from imposed restrictions and the threats of violence with which they go hand in hand. In demanding those rights for themselves, anarchists are almost duty-bound to respect those rights in others. It is here that anarchy and all other forms of political thought part company. Because anarchists believe that people are basically kind and good, as an act of faith they are able to conceive of and create revolution without violence. Other forms of political thought, lost in the cynical view of humans as bad and unchangeable, have no alternative but to resort to the immaturity of violence. Thus, unavoidably, anarchists must also promote pacifism, for if anarchists truly believe that they have the right to live their own lives, how can they permit the use of violence to deny others theirs?

However, standing against violence doesn't mean just passively standing by and letting it happen. If forced, pacifists will defend themselves and others from attack, not out of a sense of aggression or revenge, but from a need to demonstrate their strength, the strength of love. By opposing violence with a sense of love and respect, the aggressor is allowed to consider their own actions and is given the opportunity to back down. By opposing violence with violence nothing but an escalation can be achieved, nothing can be learnt, and existing values, regardless of who is the victor, remain unchallenged. Likewise with larger-scale conflict. If the State is opposed with violence, it will reply with violence, whereas if it is opposed with a desire to create love and respect, it is not impossible that love and respect could be the response. The choice is ours, it must be worth trying. The personal risk involved in rejecting violence with love is, perhaps, far higher than the traditional approach of an eye for an eye. It takes a true sense of courage to reply to violence with love rather than fists, but the rewards are real and lasting. Violence has become such an accepted method of solving problems that people justify it on the grounds that it is natural instinct. Pacifists, like anarchists, believe that our natural instinct is one of love and that violence is simply the result of that love having been stifled and perverted by repressive social systems.

From domestic violence to global war, the rules have always been the same, 'destroy that which you don't understand'. Pacifists and anarchists seek to creatively solve problems by developing mutual understanding between people rather than mutual hostility. Violence only makes disagreements worse. It works on the principle of winners and losers. Pacifists and anarchists believe that no one should have to suffer the inhuman condition of being a loser, and that no one should have to benefit from the inhuman condition of being a winner. We're not born that way, so why should we, or anyone else, live that way? All other forms of political thought rely on there being losers who are then exploited as slaves by the winners. Both right and left wing States employ force to maintain power. People are reduced to simple tools servicing the machinery of the State and as such are expected to live and if need be die for that State.

Anarchy is the rejection of State control, a demand by the individual to live a life of personal choice. Anarchists believe that if each individual can learn to act out of personal conscience rather than greed, the machinery of power will collapse. It is unfair and untrue to say that this is nothing but dreamy idealism. Throughout history people have created change without resorting to violence by simply, en masse, refusing to bow down to the authority that seeks to oppress them. History books rarely document these victories of the people because history books are concerned with the politics of power rather than the lives of the people. It is true that the State has often overthrown shows of passive resistance with violence, but had that resistance itself been of a violent nature, the State would simply have overthrown it with a greater force. Violence breeds violence. It is to cases of State violence that those who advocate armed revolution always refer when attempting to justify their own desire for violence. Never do they accept the enormous changes that have been achieved through anarcho-pacifist methods. Their deep-rooted cynicism and desire for revenge makes them blind to the strength of human goodness. These overgrown schoolboys and frustrated college

Marxists advocate armed revolution by the working classes to overthrow the oppressor. As is the usual case with macho-dominated politics, the privileged few determine the violent deaths of thousands of innocent people. The State has always sent the working classes to the front lines of war, has always used the working classes as a tool to its own power. In what way are these 'brothers' of the Marxist Revolution any different? What kind of liberation is it that uses the deaths of others, usually the underprivileged, as a means to achieve its ends?

The extreme left is largely made up from educated and privileged people who, because of their social background, are able to infiltrate organisations, from schools to the media, in which they can push their propaganda. The threat that they pose to the development of radical creative change is far greater than that of right-wing organisations. The right, because it lacks any true political ideology, or at least because that which it does have is so laughably transparent, and because it rarely has the 'social respectability' afforded to the Left, relies on its appeal to a small number of people who, finding themselves on the bottom of the social scrap-heap, rejected by leftists and liberals alike, take the only option that is on offer to them: violence. So-called 'right-wing violence' is generally not politically motivated at all, but is simply an end-of-the-line knee-jerk reaction made by people who are offered nothing by society but a life of slavery. On the other hand, the left-wing 'threat' is an organised and calculated attempt by generally privileged people who to gain power and control will use those who are less privileged to fight their causes. Those that do not conform to their leftist requirements they label as 'fascists'. At the same time, however, they would happily recruit those so-called fascists to achieve their own ends. In violence there is no morality. By simply refusing to be used as tools to other people's desires, we have the strength to overcome oppression. But do we have the personal courage to stand alone without our Party Membership Card or Little Red Book?

DO WE HAVE THE COURAGE?

If we really want to, we are able to create change immediately. We can try to live in harmony with our friends and amongst the people and the environment in which we move. We can try to be creative with the facilities that we and others make. We can learn to reject the stupid roles that we are told to accept: dominant male, submissive female etcetera. We can learn to share and cooperate with each other, to give back to life what we and others have taken from it. We can learn to understand the natural functions of the world around us: the seasons, the weather, the soil and everything that grows on this planet of ours. We can learn to understand what people, in their unthinking ways, have done to the Earth. We can learn to reject the grey lies that we are told are the facts of life. We can demand and create something better. All these things and a lot more. We can learn together with those who care and then, as individuals, we can go out into the streets and demand back the world that we know exists beneath the layer upon layer of lies that history has imposed upon it. We can start working towards something better.

NOW!

It is up to each one of us as individuals, together to subvert the System which perverts our lives. We must learn to be unafraid of those in authority. We must strive for what we know is right. Rather than simply serving our own greed and selfishness, we must find creative new ways to break the back of the System. We must write songs and poetry, make records, magazines, books, films and videos, spray messages in graffiti and attempt to gain access to all forms of media so that our voice can be heard. We must, however, be prepared to back up our words with actions.

Penny Rimbaud

GET UP AND DO IT!

It is dangerous and unwise to advocate 'direct action'. It is something that should be done and not spoken about. Each of us has our own level of fear and uncertainty. In taking direct action as a form of protest, we must be as certain as possible that we will succeed. Unless we simply want to end up as martyrs, it is foolhardy to attempt anything that we are not ready for. Rather than diving headlong into something that we find we can't carry through, we must learn to overcome our fears gradually.

In America, anarcho-pacifists broke into an air base and smashed up part of a nuclear missile. In France, they fired rockets at an unoccupied nuclear power station. In Britain, they built barriers across a railway line to prevent the transportation of nuclear waste. Other people jam up the locks of banks and offices with super-glue, or cut down fences around Government installations. Others sabotage operations at work, from redirecting traffic on building sites, to redistributing goods through the back doors of factories and shops. Everyone has their own way and their own ideas about what to do to oppose the System. Every action, however small, further erodes the power that the authorities believe they have over us. Every little helps. However, whatever it is that you do, keep your mouth shut.

THOSE WHO DO THE TALKING RARELY MAKE THE ACTIONS.

Quite apart from direct action, there are things that we can do within the existing social structures that will weaken those structures while at the same time helping ourselves and each other. We can open up squats and start information services for those who want to do the same. We can form housing co-ops and communes to share the responsibility of renting or even buying a property. In places where we already live, we can open the doors to others. We can form Tenant Associations with neighbours and demand and create better conditions and facilities in the area. We can form gardening groups that squat and farm disused land, or rent allotments where we can produce food for ourselves and others that is free from dangerous chemicals. We can grow medicinal herbs to cure each other's headaches. We can create health groups where we can practice alternative medicine, like herbalism and massage, that create healthy bodies and minds rather than the drugged-up robots that are the results of conventional medicine. Maybe we can then learn to love and respect each other's bodies rather than fearing them. We can form free schools where knowledge can be shared rather than rules laid down. Education, rather than being State training in slavery, can become a mutual growth and a true enquiry into the world around us, a place where everyone is the teacher and everyone is the pupil. We can start community centres to offer an alternative to the male dominated, money-orientated atmosphere of Britain's only nightly social event, the pub. Centres could serve and further the interests of the community rather than simply being there to finance the brewer.

For example, in Scotland, a group of anarchists found an unused site hut which they squatted. Having soundproofed and decorated it, they organised gigs and discussion groups. The Local Council were so impressed by their efforts that they have been given official use of it.

We can run food co-ops that buy and distribute foods that have been grown by people that we know, or have been brought from sources who we trust are not exploiting the people who produced it. A lot of supermarket food is grown in the Third World where the workers are paid next to nothing so that the middlemen and the supermarkets can make huge profits. Food co-ops can break down that chain. At one time we ran a food co-op from our house which supplied over twenty other homes with food that had been produced outside the capitalist system. We can form 'work banks' where we can exchange our individual skills for the skills of others. If enough people are prepared to join such a bank, money becomes almost redundant.

The only limitation is our imagination. We can overcome the structures that oppress us, but only if we are prepared to work hard to do so. We have the strength, we have the numbers and, with the courage of our own convictions, we can regain the right to live our own lives. The nonviolent revolution can, and will, be a reality.

THE REVOLUTION IS NOW.

Wally had both the strength and the courage of his own convictions, but like ourselves had been hopelessly ill-informed about the true workings of the State. He demanded the right to live his own life and was met with savage resistance. He was killed by a System that believes that it knows best. It is that System and hundreds like it that oppress millions of people throughout the world.

Left-wing oppression in Poland or right-wing oppression in Northern Ireland, what's the difference? The prisons and mental hospitals of the world are full of people who did nothing but disagree with the accepted norms of the State in which they lived. Russian dissidents are American heroes. American dissidents are Russian heroes. The kettle simply gets blacker. To defeat the oppressor we must learn its ways, otherwise, like Wally, we are doomed to be silenced by its fist.

Wally sought peace and creativity as an alternative to war and destruction. He was an anarchist, a pacifist and above all, an individualist, but because of the times in which he naively lived and innocently died he was labelled 'hippie'.

In the Coroner's Court the Police Inspector responsible for investigating Wally's death dismissed him in one sarcastic remark: 'he thought he was Jesus Christ, didn't he?' I don't think that Wally saw himself in that light, but judging by the way in which the State dealt with him, they did. The same Inspector claimed to have thoroughly interviewed everyone who had had contact with Wally from the time of his arrest to the time of his death. Although we had twice visited Wally in hospital and he had later stayed with us for around two weeks, this respectable guardian of the law had not once been in touch with us. The few witnesses that were called had obviously been carefully selected to follow the official line. Amongst them was one of the doctors who had been responsible for Wally's treatment in jail. Throughout his statement he told lie after lie and then, rather than being subjected to the possible embarrassment of cross-examination, was reminded by the coroner that he mustn't miss his train: nod, nod, wink, wink. The court passed a verdict of suicide with no reference at all to the appalling treatment that had been the direct cause of it. We loudly protested from the back of the courtroom. The grey men simply met our objections with mocking smiles.

Wally's death and the deceitful way in which the authorities dealt with it, led me to spend the next year making investigations into exactly what had happened since he left us that hot day in May. My enquiries convinced me that what had happened was not an accident. The State had intended to destroy Wally's spirit if not his life, because he was a threat, a fearless threat who they hoped they could destroy without much risk of being exposed. The story that unfolded was a nightmare web of deception, corruption and cruelty. Wally had been treated with complete contempt by the police who arrested him, the courts that sentenced him and the prison and hospital that held him prisoner. My enquiries led me far from Wally's case. As I tried to get to the truth of any one situation, I would be presented with innumerable new leads to follow. I got drawn down deeper and deeper into a world of lies, violence, greed and fear. Put simply, I was pathetically ill-prepared for what I discovered. The world started to feel like a very, very small, dark place.

I found evidence of murder cover-ups, of police and gangland tie-ups, of wrongful arrest and imprisonment on trumped up charges and false evidence. I learnt of the horrific abuse, both physical and mental, of prisoners in jails and mental hospitals, of doctors who knowingly prescribed what amounted to poison, and who were unable to see the bruises inflicted by courtesy of Her Majesty's officials on an inmate's body. I learnt of interrogating police who were ordered to punch below the head where the bruises wouldn't be seen by visiting relatives, or of jail warders who, to while the day away, set inmates against each other and did 'good turns' in return for material and sexual favours. I learnt of nurses in mental hospitals who deliberately administered the wrong drugs to patients 'just to see what happened', and who, for kicks, tied patients to their beds and then tormented them or quite simply raped them. The official line, that the purpose of prisons is reform and of mental hospitals is cure, is total deception. The purpose is punishment. Punishment by revenge: savage, unthinking, brutal.

Beyond the world of police, courts, jails and asylums, I was faced with the perhaps even more sickening outside world. Within this world, respectable people, smart and secure, work day in and day out to maintain the lie. They know about the abuse and cruelty, they know about the dishonesty and corruption, they know about the complete falsity of the reality in which they live, but they daren't turn against it because, having invested so much of their lives in it, they would be turning against themselves. So they remain silent. They are the silent, violent, majority. Beneath the glossy surfaces of neatly combed hair and straightened nylons, of polished cars and sponged-down cookers, of pub on Friday and occasional church on Sunday, of well-planned family and better-planned future, of wealth and security, of power and glory, they are the real fascists. They know, but they remain silent.

> 'First they came for the Jews and I did not speak out because I was not a Jew. Then they came for the communists and I did not speak out because I was not a communist. Then they came for the trade unionists and I did not speak out because I was not a trade unionist. Then they came for me, and there was no one left to speak out for me.'
> —Pastor Niemoeller, victim of the Nazis

They remain silent when the windows of the house across the street are smashed and the walls daubed with racist abuse. Silent when they hear the footsteps at night and the beating of doors and the sobbing of those inside. Now perhaps they whisper one to the other, the quietest whisper: 'they're only Jews, you know,' or Catholics, West Indians, Pakistanis, Indians, Arabs, Chinese, Irish, Gypsies, gays, cripples, or any minority group, in any society, anywhere. They only whisper it once before the warmth of the duck-down continental quilt soothes away their almost accidental guilt. Silent again as they hear them led away into the darkness. Silent, as through the cold mist of morning, they hear the cattle-trucks roll by. And when they hear of the death-pits, of the racks, of the ovens, of the millions dead and millions dying, they remain silent. Because security is their god and compliance is his mistress, they remain silent. Against all the evidence, against all that they know, they remain silent, Silent because convention decrees that they should be silent. Silence, security, compliance and convention: the roots of fascism. Their passive silence is their active part in the violence, a huge and powerful, silent voice of approval: the voice of fascism.

It is not the National Front or the British Movement that represents the real right-wing threat. Like the dinosaurs before them, they are all body and no brain and because of that they will become extinct. It is the general public, the silent majority, who, in their willingness to bow down to authority, pose the real fascist threat. Fascism is as much in the hearts of the people as in the minds of their potential leaders.

THE GAG IS ON THE HEART AND SOUL.

It was these voices of silence which at times made my investigations into Wally's death almost impossible. The respectable majority were too concerned about their own security to want to risk upsetting the authorities by telling me what they knew. They did know and I knew that they knew, but it made no difference. They remained silent.

From the enormous file of documentation that my enquiries produced, I compiled a lengthy book on the life and death of Wally Hope. During my enquiries I had received two death-threats and had been visited several times by the police who softly, softly let me know that they knew what I knew and that they wanted me to remain silent. I felt alone and vulnerable. Sick of what I had learnt and fearful of what I might yet learn, one fine spring morning my nerve finally gave out. One and a half years after Wally's death, I threw the book and almost all the documentation onto a bonfire and watched the flames leap into the perfect blue sky.

Phil Russell was at last dead.

I had never chosen to be a part of the System. From an early age I had decided to live my own life in my own way. For years it seemed to work. Wally had come along at a time when I was beginning to question the value of what I was doing. Was it enough? My experiences both before and after his death showed me that it wasn't. I had been prepared to believe that the System wasn't all bad, that if I acted honestly with it, it would act honestly with me. At the time, however, I still naively believed that the System served the people. My experiences showed me that, in fact, it was the people who served the System . . . or else.

I had tried to demonstrate my sense of freedom with humour and love, and was met with violence and hate, which in turn I attempted to combat with reason and intelligence. I failed. I finally realised that the State, those who work for it and those who live beneath its authority, were the enemy of our freedom and that we must look for other ways than well-reasoned words with which to oppose them. The System has at its command everything that it needs to control the people and to ensure that its conditions remain dominant. It has the family to limit movement and stabilise those conditions. It has schools to restrict the mind and brainwash with those conditions. It has employment and taxation of it to finance the authorities that maintain those conditions. It has the law, the courts and the police to enforce those conditions. It has the army to protect those conditions. It has prisons and mental hospitals to punish anyone who disobeys those conditions. It has the media to promote those conditions. It has Royalty to flaunt those conditions. It has religion and psychiatry to mystify and thereby threaten at the deepest level those who question those conditions. It has history and tradition to prove the value of those conditions. It has the future in which all these things are employed to ensure that those conditions will remain unchallenged.

WE HAVE NOTHING BUT OURSELVES AND EACH OTHER.

The System quietly murders people like Wally, yet still it is respected by the majority. The System openly murders people like Blair Peach, yet still it is respected by the majority. The System noisily murders people like Bobby Sands, yet still it is respected by the majority. The System is prepared to wage vicious civil war, as in Northern Ireland, or to consider the horror of total annihilation in a global nuclear war, yet still it is respected by the majority. The System and all those who support it, either directly or through silence, are guilty of premeditating the deaths of millions of people, from individuals like Wally, to the nameless, unidentifiable masses in some unspeakable war. They are guilty of conspiring to destroy the planet, the people, animals, insects, plants, in fact everything that we know as life. There, in their seats of power, hidden behind their masks of reason and rationale, sit people who are not only prepared to destroy our world, but are proud to admit it. It is these self-confessed potential mass-murderers whom we permit to rule our lives. It is these dangerous fools who are the real mad people, not gentle visionaries like Wally. Yet who is it who is punished in this reality of double-standards and hypocrisy? We know that they are not fit to rule our world, yet we allow them to do so. We allow them to build around us a hideously dangerous environment. Britain is at risk of becoming little more than a launch-pad for American missiles and a practice ground for Russian ones. Thatcher's Government intends to spend twelve and a half thousand million pounds this year, 1982, on the military alone, and that doesn't include the other thousands of millions on war related expenses, from communication systems to Government fall-out shelters and nuclear power stations. The British coastline is becoming dotted with potentially lethal nuclear power stations that produce very little electricity, about ten per cent of yearly UK requirements, and very big bombs. The first power stations were built solely for the production of nuclear bombs. There is little to suggest that those being built now are for anything but similar purposes.

The air, the sea and the land are becoming increasingly polluted with nuclear waste. The Irish Sea is the most radioactive stretch of water in the world. People, animals, birds, fish and plants have already died as a result of this mindless litter-bugging. Do we have to wait for the accident that will and must happen, that kills people by the thousands, before the authorities accept that there is a little bit more at risk than their self-important reputations? The nuclear programme has enabled the authorities to enormously intensify the development of so-called 'security systems'. So not only do we have to suffer the insecurity of the threat of nuclear war, we also have to contend with the added insecurity of living in what is fast becoming a Police State. Nuclear establishments have at their command an armed force who answer to no authority but their own. They are Britain's ready-made SS, existing as a State within a State.

The Government recently approved plans to set up a new-style 'Home Guard', a force who will be specially trained to deal with 'domestic problems', and that means me and you. So don't be fooled by tales of Dad's Army. This one isn't a comedy. The authorities are increasingly prying into our private lives. From phone tapping to census forms, our lives are becoming files in their dark offices. The authorities have just purchased a computer system capable of linking together all the other computers that store information about every man, woman and child living in Britain. At the press of a button, the authorities will be able to have details on our lives, from birth to the present time. It is not impossible that in time they might also be predicting what it is we are about to do.

Fifteen years ago, I was claiming that computers were going to enormously limit individual freedom. Naturally, I was accused of being paranoid, but nonetheless, that is exactly what they are now doing. With the development of the 'micro chip' there is no way that anyone could imagine the effects that these new technologies will have on our privacy and freedom. Orwell's 1984 has become a memory two years before its sell-by date, a clumsy hypothesis that fell hopelessly short in its failure to allow for the horrific escalation in technological 'hardware'.

Private life is becoming something of the past. We are becoming nothing but numbers in some bizarre lottery game, and when your number is called, run like the devil. But beware, they'll probably have a print-out on exactly where it is that you're running to.

> *'Just because they say you're paranoid doesn't mean that you're not stored in their computers.'*
>
> —Well-known punk wit

As the authorities increase military expenditure, the money for the so-called Social Services is decreased. We are expected to live on less and less as the Government spends more and more on their war games. In Great Britain, 1982, there are people who are suffering from malnutrition because they can't afford food, they are freezing to death because they can't afford heat, they are being made homeless because they can't afford the rent, they are being moved into half-way houses because Councils can't afford decent homes and where they are suffering from malnutrition because they can't afford food and freezing to death because they can't afford heat. Round and round and round again. And when the deprivation finally makes them ill, they are being moved into hospitals where the authorities can't afford to properly treat them. They'll probably die young, but, hey, most people die eventually anyway. Meanwhile, this year, 1982, Her Majesty's Government is spending twelve and a half thousand million pounds on the military alone and that doesn't include the other thousands of millions on war-related expenses, from communications systah, blah,

hello, hello, is anybody still there?

In Northern Ireland, citizens pay Government taxes so that Government forces can remain there in occupation, If just half of what was spent on maintaining those forces was spent on redeveloping the housing, the social facilities, and most importantly, the trust that those forces have destroyed, maybe a solution would be a little easier to find.

But of course the Government is not looking for a real solution, it is looking for a way in which it can continue its exploitation of the people and the land without opposition from any of the rival factions. The army in Northern Ireland is not a peace-keeping force whatever the Government may say. It is an army of occupation and all the people, be they Catholic, Protestant or indifferent, suffer accordingly. It was the English who created the Irish Problem when hundreds of years ago they first invaded Ireland for exactly the same reasons that since then they have invaded countless countries throughout the world: to exploit natural assets. As long as those assets continue to profit Westminster, the Irish Problem will exist. Young men whose only difference is the narrow strip of water, or perhaps more tragic still, the narrow strip of land that divides their birthplaces, shoot at each other across an atmosphere of accumulated hatred. Yet what can they know to hate this way?

They know nothing but what they have been told to know by the authorities, those who care nothing for their deaths but what they might gain by them. See how Paper Tiger Thatcher cried crocodile tears for her lost son, yet see how little compassion she had for the families of the H Block dead. Centuries of wasted blood. Centuries of wasted tears. Each vessel another childless mother. Each death another stupid reprisal. When will we ever learn? When will we ever learn?

NEWSFLASH!!!

Over the last few weeks, Britain has gone to war in the Falklands, graphically illustrating the complete madness of Margaret Thatcher and her Government. What should have been little more than a minor territorial dispute requiring discussion and diplomacy has blown up into a tense world situation where hundreds of young men have already died for the arrogance of their leaders.

Around one hundred and fifty years ago, the British stole the Falklands so that they could maintain access into the Pacific Ocean. Since that time the Argentineans have made repeated attempts to negotiate a return of the islands to their control. Had it not been for the access it gave to possible oil and mineral deposits in the area, Britain would have handed back the islands without a second thought. Eventually, and inevitably, the Argentineans reinvaded the Falklands and Thatcher's Government, seizing it as an opportunity to divert attention from its enormous domestic problems, launched the country into war. Nonetheless, however understandable the Argentinean aggression might be, it remains as unacceptable as the British response. Violence breeds violence.

Historically Britain has no right to the Falklands. It seems easy to criticise the Argentinean action, yet it was precisely those methods that Britain used to steal the islands in the first place. Let's get real about this, Thatcher, her Government and other Governments before her couldn't give a toss for the British people who live on the island. Nor do they care about 'sovereignty'. It is the possibility of oil and minerals that they care about, the wealth and the power that they can exploit, and if that means that hundreds of people are going to die, tough, or as Thatcher so neatly put it, 'rejoice'. The nationalistic fervour that this nasty little skirmish has whipped up is just a crude cover which enables Thatcher to send young men to premature death and to create an atmosphere in which it becomes acceptable to brutally murder the so-called enemy. Thatcher talks of peaceful solutions whilst ordering the slaughter of five hundred young men. She claims that 'our people' need protection whilst already having been responsible for the murder of over thirty of them. She is a bigot, a hypocrite and a liar.

To keep the jingoistic blood on the boil, obscene articles appear daily in the press. The dehumanising term 'Argie' has been coined to make the death and mutilation of fellow human beings appear commonplace and ordinary. Page three pin-ups have appeared wearing an assortment of nationalistic insults. Desperate sweethearts flashed their knickers as the QE2 sailed away with its cargo of gun-fodder. Britain relived the war years, rallying to its bloodstained flag in some dreadful memory of a power that once held half the world in its steely imperialist grip. Now that grip has become no more than a weak-wristed fantasy which through sheer arrogance would risk the safety of the whole planet. How long must young men continue to die for the greed of governments? How long must young women exploit their bodies to support this psycho-sexual fantasy of war? The big bang, big fuck. When are we going to learn to say 'no' and to really mean it?

Through their massive taxation of us, the Government finances its oppression of us. Northern Ireland has been a training ground for what the authorities fear is going to happen on the mainland. As the dividing line between those who can afford and those who can't grows, and as jobs become increasingly difficult to find and increasingly boring and pointless when they are found, so the overall quality of life deteriorates and the reasons for supporting those who are responsible for it become meaningless. As long as those who are in power can command the loyalty of the general public whom they regard as slaves, they will continue to use the general public to abuse the general public. The rich will get richer and the general public will be left to fight amongst themselves.

Cities, where the vast majority of the population live and work, are becoming hostile islands of grey concrete where carbon monoxide poisons the air, where unbridled commercial development makes housing almost impossible to find, and increasingly derelict when it is found, where the streets are not somewhere where you look for friends, but somewhere where you hide from enemies, where people are too scared to look each other in the eyes, where people only stop when the colourful posters or seductive shop window-displays demand that they should. We are teased and titillated. Buy this, buy that. The ad-men and the glitzy models exploit and manipulate. Buy this, buy that. Consume, consume, consume. The parasites become wealthy at the expense of the general public, but the parasites are the general public. The serpent eats its own tail. The glossy advertisements are almost pointless. They're way above our heads. Who can afford this trash? But all the same, those who can afford, buy, and those who can't, resent it. Buy this, buy that. On all kinds of levels, the posters and billboards aim to make us feel inadequate.

You're not a man unless . . . You're not a woman unless . . . Unless? Unless what?

TIA MARIA?
NICE IDEA!

Nice idea maybe, but who can afford the sun-drenched pool in St. Tropez? Who can conform to the standard fantasy norms of sexuality that those glitzy models so gracelessly display? Is mine big enough? Who can afford the drink, let alone the life style? But all the same, those who can afford, buy and those who can't get angry. Buy this, buy that. So, we are forced to accept second best to that which the System tells us we should aspire. We are told that to belong we must conform to certain social stereotypes yet, at the same time, the System which creates those stereotypes knows perfectly well that very few people can actually afford the necessary credentials. The media creates and promotes standards of requirement, from video-games to holidays in the Seychelles, that only the privileged few could hope to afford. Those who can't afford, but nonetheless want to conform, are left confused, belittled, and alienated. But all the same, those who can afford, buy, and those who can't finally explode into a frenzy of hatred and revenge and smash the seductive shop windows and take the things from the people who have manipulated them into believing that these are the things that they want. Buy this, buy that. Take this, take that.

TIT FOR TAT.

So as Brixton, Toxteth and Moss Side burn, the System closes in to strengthen its grip and controls get tighter. The police are given even greater powers, and the army, fresh from the training grounds of Belfast and Derry, wait in the shadows. The Government, those in authority, and all those who serve and support them, are placing the people in an impossible stranglehold.

The age of consumerism, born out of the horror and guilt of World War Two, has failed to live up to its promise. Neither a Cadillac nor a super deluxe washing-machine make the threat of annihilation any more acceptable. For a while they might have made it a little more bearable, but now the threat has become too real to be hidden by layers of consumer junk which, in any case, very few people can afford.

The authorities have lost their bargaining power. They no longer have anything to offer in exchange for the sacrifices that they ask us to make, so they're no longer asking us, they're telling us. They're telling us to work for things that we can't afford so that they can run the System that, without us and the money we make and they take, they can't afford. As the System increasingly realises its failure, it strengthens the barriers that exist between them and us with all the authority that it can command. But the only authority that they command is us, so who are they?

At last, we have reached a turning point.

Authority does not exist without the value and support that we give it. As long as we, the people, bow down to the System, authority will exist and so will the System. Either we accept that we are to live as mindless robots in a world that is walking the tightrope of nuclear war, where security checks will become a way of life, where the streets are patrolled by tanks and the skies by helicopters, where people no longer dare speak of what they believe for fear of those who might be listening, where love is a memory, peace a dream and freedom simply does not exist, or we demand our rights, refuse to be a part of the authority that denies them, and recognise that the System is nothing but a small handful of ruling elites who are powerless without our support.

We have the **strength,**butdowe have the **courage?**

We must learn to live with our own **weakness, hatred and prejudice,** and to reject theirs.

We must learn to live with our own **fears, doubts and inadequacies,** and to reject theirs.

We must learn to live with our own **love, passion and desire,** and to reject theirs.

We must learn to live with our own **conscience, awareness and certainty,** and to reject theirs.

We must learn to live with our own **moralities, values and standards,** and to reject theirs.

We must learn to live with our own **principles, ethics and philosophies,** and to reject theirs.

Above all, we must learn to live with our own **strength** and learn how to use it against them as they have used it against us.

Throughout history, it is our **strength** that they have used against us to maintain their **privileged** positions.

It is up to me alone, and you alone, to **bite the hand that bleeds us.**

THERE IS NO FUTURE BUT OUR OWN.

YOU AND I, WHO LOVE THIS PLANET EARTH, ARE ITS RIGHTFUL INHERITORS.

THERE IS
NO AUTHORITY
BUT
OUR
OWN.

IT IS
TIME
TO STAKE
OUR CLAIM.

Throughout the hippie era I had championed the cause of peace. I had joined some of the first CND marches and later, with great sadness, I had watched the Peace Movement being eroded by political greed. Throughout the 'drop out and cop out' period I hung on to the belief that real change could only come about through personal example. I had hoped that through a practical demonstration of peace and love I would be able to paint the grey world in new colours. It is ironic that it took a man called Hope, the only real hippie with whom I ever became directly creatively involved, to show me that that particular form of hope was a dream. The experiences I gained through my friendship with Wally led me realise that it was time to have a rethink about the way in which I should pursue my vision of peace. Wally's death showed me that I could not afford to sit by and let it happen again. In part, his death was my responsibility, and although I did everything that I could, it was not enough.

Desire for change had to be coupled with the desire to work for it. If it was worth opposing the System, it was worth opposing it totally. It was no longer good enough to take what I wanted and to reject the rest. It was time to get into the streets and fight back.

A year after Wally's death, the Sex Pistols released 'Anarchy in the UK'. Maybe they didn't really mean it ma'am, but to me it was a battle cry. When Rotten proclaimed that there was 'no future', I saw it as a challenge to my creativity. I knew that there was a future if I was prepared to work for it. It is our world, it is ours and it has been stolen from us. I set out to demand it back, only this time round they didn't call me a dirty hippie . . .

. . . they called me a filthy punk.

ABOUT PENNY RIMBAUD

PENNY RIMBAUD IS A WRITER, POET, PHILOSOPHER, painter, musician and activist. He was a former member of the performance art groups EXIT and Ceres Confusion, and in 1972 was cofounder with Phil Russell (aka Wally Hope) of the Stonehenge Free Festivals. In 1977, alongside Steve Ignorant, he cofounded the seminal anarchist punk band Crass, which disbanded in 1984. From that time up until 2000 he devoted himself almost entirely to writing, returning to the public platform in 2001 as a performance poet working alongside Australian saxophonist Louise Elliott and a wide variety of jazz musicians under the umbrella of Penny Rimbaud's Last Amendment.

About PM Press

politics • culture • art • fiction • music • film

PM Press was founded at the end of 2007 by a small collection of folks with decades of publishing, media, and organizing experience. PM Press co-conspirators have published and distributed hundreds of books, pamphlets, CDs, and DVDs. Members of PM have founded enduring book fairs, spearheaded victorious tenant organizing campaigns, and worked closely with bookstores, academic conferences, and even rock bands to deliver political and challenging ideas to all walks of life. We're old enough to know what we're doing and young enough to know what's at stake.

We seek to create radical and stimulating fiction and nonfiction books, pamphlets, T-shirts, visual and audio materials to entertain, educate, and inspire you. We aim to distribute these through every available channel with every available technology, whether that means you are seeing anarchist classics at our bookfair stalls; reading our latest vegan cookbook at the café; downloading geeky fiction e-books; or digging new music and timely videos from our website.

Contact us for direct ordering and questions about all PM Press releases, as well as manuscript submissions, review copy requests, foreign rights sales, author interviews, to book an author for an event, and to have PM Press attend your bookfair:

PM Press • PO Box 23912 • Oakland, CA 94623
510-658-3906 • info@pmpress.org

Buy books and stay on top of what we are doing at:

www.pmpress.org

MONTHLY SUBSCRIPTION PROGRAM

These are indisputably momentous times—the financial system is melting down globally and the Empire is stumbling. Now more than ever there is a vital need for radical ideas.

In the eight years since its founding—and on a mere shoestring—PM Press has risen to the formidable challenge of publishing and distributing knowledge and entertainment for the struggles ahead. With hundreds of releases to date, we have published an impressive and stimulating array of literature, art, music, politics, and culture. Using every available medium, we've succeeded in connecting those hungry for ideas and information to those putting them into practice.

Friends of PM allows you to directly help impact, amplify, and revitalize the discourse and actions of radical writers, filmmakers, and artists. It provides us with a stable foundation from which we can build upon our early successes and provides a much-needed subsidy for the materials that can't necessarily pay their own way. You can help make that happen—and receive every new title automatically delivered to your door once a month—by joining as a Friend of PM Press. And, we'll throw in a free T-Shirt when you sign up.

Here are your options (all include a 50% discount on the webstore):
- $30 a month: Get all books and pamphlets
- $40 a month: Get all PM Press releases (including CDs and DVDs)
- $100 a month: Superstar—Everything plus PM merch, free downloads

For those who can't afford $30 or more a month, we're introducing **Sustainer Rates** at $15, $10, and $5. Sustainers get a free PM Press T-shirt and a 50% discount on all purchases from our website.

Your Visa or Mastercard will be billed once a month, until you tell us to stop. Or until our efforts succeed in bringing the revolution around. Or the financial meltdown of Capital makes plastic redundant. Whichever comes first.

Also Available from PM Press

The Story of Crass
George Berger
ISBN: 978-1-60486-037-5
$20.00

The Primal Screamer
Nick Blinko
ISBN: 978-1-60486-331-4
$14.95

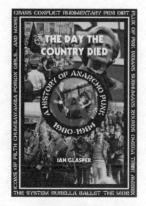

The Day the Country Died
A History of Anarcho
Punk 1980–1984
Ian Glasper
ISBN: 978-1-60486-516-5
$24.95

A Mix of Bricks
& Valentines
Lyrics 1979–2009
G.W. Sok
ISBN: 978-1-60486-499-1
$20.00

Also Available from PM Press

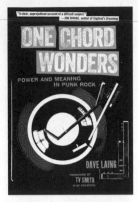

One Chord Wonders
Power and Meaning
in Punk Rock
Dave Laing
ISBN: 978-1-62963-033-5
$17.95

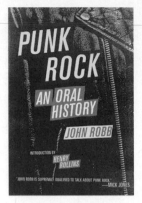

Punk Rock
An Oral History
John Robb
ISBN: 978-1-60486-005-4
$19.95

Burning Britain
The History of UK
Punk 1980–1984
Ian Glasper
ISBN: 978-1-60486-748-0
$24.95

Dead Kennedys
Fresh Fruit for Rotting
Vegetables, The Early Years
Alex Ogg
ISBN: 978-1-60486-489-2
$17.95